THE PELICAN SHAKESPEARE
GENERAL EDITORS

STEPHEN ORGEL
A. R. BRAUNMULLER

The Tragedy of King Richard the Third

Richard wooing Lady Anne (I.2). The consummate villain
Edmund Kean (1789–1833) in one of his two most
famous roles—the other was Iago.

William Shakespeare

The Tragedy of
King Richard the Third

EDITED BY PETER HOLLAND

PENGUIN BOOKS

PENGUIN BOOKS

An imprint of Penguin Random House LLC
375 Hudson Street
New York, New York 10014
penguin.com

The Tragedy of King Richard the Third edited by G. Blakemore Evans
published in Penguin Books (USA) 1959
Revised edition published 1969
Edition edited by Peter Holland published 2000
This edition published 2017

ISBN 9780143130253

Printed in the United States of America

Set in Adobe Garamond
Designed by Virginia Norey

Contents

Publisher's Note

THE PELICAN SHAKESPEARE has served generations of readers as an authoritative series of texts and scholarship since the first volume appeared under the general editorship of Alfred Harbage over half a century ago. In the past decades, new editions followed to reflect the profound changes textual and critical studies of Shakespeare have undergone. The texts of the plays and poems were thoroughly revised in accordance with leading scholarship, and in some cases were entirely reedited. New introductions and notes were provided in all the volumes. The Pelican Shakespeare was designed as a successor to the original series; the previous editions had been taken into account, and the advice of the previous editors was solicited where it was feasible to do so. The current editions include updated bibliographic references to recent scholarship.

Certain textual features of the new Pelican Shakespeare should be particularly noted. All lines are numbered that contain a word, phrase, or allusion explained in the glossarial notes. In addition, for convenience, every tenth line is also numbered, in italics when no annotation is indicated. The intrusive and often inaccurate place headings inserted by early editors are omitted (as has become standard practice), but for the convenience of those who miss them, an indication of locale now appears as the first item in the annotation of each scene.

In the interest of both elegance and utility, each speech prefix is set in a separate line when the speakers' lines are in verse, except when those words form the second half of a verse line. Thus the verse form of the speech is kept visually intact. What is printed as verse and what is printed as prose has, in general, the authority of the original texts. Departures from the original texts in this regard have the authority only of editorial tradition and the judgment of the Pelican editors; and, in a few instances, are admittedly arbitrary.

The Theatrical World

ECONOMIC REALITIES determined the theatrical world in which Shakespeare's plays were written, performed, and received. For centuries in England, the primary theatrical tradition was nonprofessional. Craft guilds (or "mysteries") provided religious drama – mystery plays – as part of the celebration of religious and civic festivals, and schools and universities staged classical and neoclassical drama in both Latin and English as part of their curricula. In these forms, drama was established and socially acceptable. Professional theater, in contrast, existed on the margins of society. The acting companies were itinerant; playhouses could be any available space – the great halls of the aristocracy, town squares, civic halls, inn yards, fair booths, or open fields – and income was sporadic, dependent on the passing of the hat or on the bounty of local patrons. The actors, moreover, were considered little better than vagabonds, constantly in danger of arrest or expulsion.

In the late 1560s and 1570s, however, English professional theater began to gain respectability. Wealthy aristocrats fond of drama – the Lord Admiral, for example, or the Lord Chamberlain – took acting companies under their protection so that the players technically became members of their households and were no longer subject to arrest as homeless or masterless men. Permanent theaters were first built at this time as well, allowing the companies to control and charge for entry to their performances.

Shakespeare's livelihood, and the stunning artistic explosion in which he participated, depended on pragmatic and architectural effort. Professional theater requires ways to restrict access to its offerings; if it does not, and admission fees cannot be charged, the actors do not get paid, the costumes go to a pawnbroker, and there is no such thing as a professional, ongoing theatrical tradition. The answer to that economic need arrived in the late 1560s and 1570s with the creation of the so-called public or amphitheater playhouse. Recent discoveries indicate that the precursor of the Globe playhouse in London (where Shakespeare's mature plays were presented) and the Rose theater (which presented Christopher Marlowe's plays and some of Shakespeare's earliest ones) was the Red Lion theater of 1567.

Extensive parts of the foundations of the Rose theater, apparently the fourth public theater to be built, were uncovered in 1989. A few years later, a much smaller portion of the second Globe (rebuilt after the first burned in 1613) was located. The remains of the Rose indicate that it originally (1587) had a rather small "thrust" stage that tapered into the open area from which a standing audience, the "groundlings," watched. The stage was approximately 25 feet wide at the front, more than 36 feet wide at the back, and about 16½ feet deep; it was placed at the northern end of a north-south axis, presumably to maximize the amount of light falling on the stage during the spring-summer playing season. In early 1592, the Rose's owner, Philip Henslowe, paid to renovate and expand his theater; the new stage was at least 18 feet deep, perhaps more if the stage boards projected out over the newly laid brick foundations. The seating area also increased, but both theater and stage remained relatively small compared to the rectangular stage at the Fortune (1600), over 40 feet wide and supposedly based upon the Globe. The Globe building may have been as much as 100 feet in diameter, while the Rose's diameter was about 72 feet. Both theaters were irregular polygons, multistoried, with areas for the groundlings, and with a covered gallery that seated perhaps 2,200 (Rose) or 3,000 (Globe) very crowded spectators.

These theaters might have been about half full on any given day, though the audiences were larger on holidays or when a play was advertised, as old and new were, through printed playbills posted around London. The metropolitan area's late-Tudor, early-Stuart population (circa 1590–1620) has been estimated at about 150,000 to 250,000. It has been supposed that in the mid-1590s there were about 15,000 spectators per week at the public theaters; thus, as many as 10 percent of the local population went to the theater regularly. Consequently, the theaters' repertories – the plays available for this experienced and frequent audience – had to change often: in the month between September 15 and October 15, 1595, for instance, the Lord Admiral's Men performed twenty-eight times in eighteen different plays.

Since natural light illuminated the amphitheaters' stages, performances began between noon and two o'clock and ran without a break for two or three hours. They often concluded with a jig, a fencing display, or some other nondramatic exhibition. Weather conditions determined the season for the amphitheaters: plays were performed every day (including Sundays, sometimes, to clerical dismay) except during Lent – the forty days before Easter – or periods of plague, or sometimes during the summer months when law courts were not in session and the most affluent members of the audience were not in London.

To a modern theatergoer, an amphitheater stage like that of the Rose or Globe would appear an unfamiliar mixture of plainness and elaborate decoration. Much of the structure was carved or painted, sometimes to imitate marble; elsewhere, as under the canopy projecting over the stage, to represent the stars and the zodiac. Appropriate painted canvas pictures (of Jerusalem, for example, if the play was set in that city) were apparently hung on the wall behind the acting area, and tragedies were accompanied by black hangings, presumably something like crepe festoons or bunting. Although these theaters did not employ what we would call scenery, early modern spectators saw numerous large props, such as the "bar" at which a prisoner stood during a trial, the "mossy bank" where lovers reclined, an arbor for amorous conversation, a chariot, gallows, tables, trees, beds, thrones, writing desks, and so forth. Audiences might learn a scene's location from a sign (reading "Athens," for example) carried across the stage (as in Bertolt Brecht's twentieth-century productions). Equally captivating (and equally irritating to the theater's enemies) were the rich costumes and personal props the actors used: the most valuable items in the surviving theatrical inventories are the swords, gowns, robes, crowns, and other items worn or carried by the performers.

Magic appealed to Shakespeare's audiences as much as it does to us today, and the theater exploited many deceptive and spectacular devices. A winch in the loft above the stage, called "the heavens," could lower and raise actors playing gods, goddesses, and other supernatural figures to and from the main acting area, just as one or more trapdoors permitted entrances and exits to and from the area, called "hell," beneath the stage. Actors wore elementary makeup such as wigs, false beards, and face paint, and they employed pigs' bladders filled with animal blood to make wounds seem more real. They had rudimentary but effective ways of pretending to behead or hang a person. Supernumeraries (stagehands or actors not needed in a particular scene) could make thunder sounds (by shaking a metal sheet or rolling an iron ball down a chute) and show lightning (by blowing inflammable resin through tubes into a flame). Elaborate fireworks enhanced the effects of dragons flying through the air or imitated such celestial phenomena as comets, shooting stars, and multiple suns. Horses' hoofbeats, bells (located perhaps in the tower above the stage), trumpets and drums, clocks, cannon shots and gunshots, and the like were common sound effects. And the music of viols, cornets, oboes, and recorders was a regular feature of theatrical performances.

For two relatively brief spans, from the late 1570s to 1590 and from 1599 to 1614, the amphitheaters competed with the so-called private, or indoor, theaters, which originated as, or later represented themselves as, educational institutions training boys as singers for church services and court performances. These indoor theaters had two features that were distinct from the amphitheaters': their personnel and their playing spaces. The amphitheaters' adult companies included both adult men, who played the male roles, and boys, who played the female roles; the private, or indoor, theater companies, on the other hand, were entirely composed of boys aged about eight to sixteen, who were, or could pretend to be, candidates for singers in a church or a royal boys' choir. (Until 1660, professional theatrical companies included no women.) The playing space would appear much more familiar to modern audiences than the long-vanished amphitheaters; the later indoor theaters were, in fact, the ancestors of the typical modern theater. They were enclosed spaces, usually rectangular, with the stage filling one end of the rectangle and the audience arrayed in seats or benches across (and sometimes lining) the building's longer axis. These spaces staged plays less frequently than the public theaters (perhaps only once a week) and held far fewer spectators than the amphitheaters: about 200 to 600, as opposed to 2,500 or more. Fewer patrons mean a smaller gross income, unless each pays more. Not surprisingly, then, private theaters charged higher prices than the amphitheaters, probably sixpence, as opposed to a penny for the cheapest entry to the amphitheaters.

Protected from the weather, the indoor theaters presented plays later in the day than the amphitheaters, and used artificial illumination – candles in sconces or candelabra. But candles melt and need replacing, snuffing, and trimming, and these practical requirements may have been part of the reason the indoor theaters introduced breaks in the performance, the intermission so dear to the hearts of theatergoers and to the pocketbooks of theater concessionaires ever since. Whether motivated by the need to tend to the candles or by the entrepreneurs' wish to sell oranges and liquor, or both, the indoor theaters eventually established the modern convention of noncontinuous performance. In the early modern "private" theater, musical performances apparently filled the intermissions, which in Stuart theater jargon seem to have been called "acts."

At the end of the first decade of the seventeenth century, the distinction between public amphitheaters and private indoor companies ceased. For various cultural, political, and economic reasons, individual companies gained control of both the public, open-air theaters and the indoor ones, and companies mixing adult men and boys took over the formerly "private" theaters. Despite the death of the boys' companies and of their highly innovative theaters (for which such luminous playwrights as Ben Jonson, George Chapman, and John Marston wrote), their playing spaces and conventions had an immense impact on subsequent plays: not merely for the intervals (which stressed the artistic and architectonic importance of "acts"), but also because they introduced political and social satire as a popular dramatic ingredient, even in tragedy, and a wider range of actorly effects, encouraged by the more intimate playing spaces.

Even the briefest sketch of the Shakespearean theatrical world would be incomplete without some comment on the social and cultural dimensions of theaters and playing in the period. In an intensely hierarchical and status-conscious society, professional actors and their ventures had hardly any respectability; as we have indicated, to protect themselves against laws designed to curb vagabondage and the increase of masterless men, actors resorted to the near-fiction that they were the servants of noble masters and wore their distinctive livery. Hence the company for which Shakespeare wrote in the 1590s that called itself the Lord Chamberlain's Men and pretended that the public, money-getting performances were in fact rehearsals for private performances before that high court official. From 1598, the Privy Council had licensed theatrical companies, and after 1603, with the accession of King James I, the companies gained explicit royal protection, just as the Queen's Men had for a time under Queen Elizabeth. The Chamberlain's Men became the King's Men, and the other companies were patronized by other members of the royal family.

These designations were legal fictions that half-concealed an important economic and social development, the evolution away from the theater's organization on the model of the guild, a self-regulating confraternity of individual artisans, into a proto-capitalist organization. Shakespeare's company became a joint-stock company, where persons who supplied capital and, in some cases, such as Shakespeare's, capital and talent, employed themselves and others in earning a return on that capital. This development meant that actors and theater companies were outside both the traditional guild structures, which required some form of civic or royal charter, and the feudal household organization of master-and-servant. This anomalous, maverick social and economic condition made theater companies practically unruly and potentially even dangerous; consequently, numerous official bodies – including the London metropolitan and ecclesiastical authorities as well as, occasionally, the royal court itself – tried, without much success, to control and even to disband them.

Public officials had good reason to want to close the theaters: they were attractive nuisances – they drew often-riotous crowds, they were always noisy, and they could be politically offensive and socially insubordinate. Until the Civil War, however, antitheatrical forces failed to shut down professional theater, for many reasons – limited surveillance and few police powers, tensions or outright hostilities among the agencies that sought to check or channel theatrical activity, and lack of clear policies for control. Another reason must have been the theaters' undeniable popularity. Curtailing any activity enjoyed by such a substantial percentage of the population was difficult, as various Roman emperors attempting to limit circuses had learned, and the Tudor-Stuart audience was not merely large, it was socially diverse and included women. The prevalence of public entertainment in this period has been underestimated. In fact, fairs, holidays, games, sporting events, the equivalent of modern parades, freak shows, and street exhibitions all abounded, but the theater was the most widely and frequently available entertainment to which people of every class had access. That fact helps account both for its quantity and for the fear and anger it aroused.

Books About Shakespeare's Theater

Useful scholarly studies of theatrical life in Shakespeare's day include: G. E. Bentley, *The Jacobean and Caroline Stage*, 7 vols. (1941–68), and the same author's *The Professions of Dramatist and Player in Shakespeare's Time, 1590–1642* (1986); Julian Bowsher, *The Rose Theatre: An Archaeological Discovery* (1998); E. K. Chambers, *The Elizabethan Stage*, 4 vols. (1923); Christine Eccles, *The Rose Theatre* (1990); R. A. Foakes, *Illustrations of the English Stage, 1580–1642* (1985); Andrew Gurr, *The Shakespearean Stage, 1574–1642*, 3rd ed. (1992), and the same author's *Play-going in Shakespeare's London*, 2nd ed. (1996); Roslyn Lander Knutson, *Playing Companies and Commerce in Shakespeare's Time* (2001); Edwin Nungezer, *A Dictionary of Actors* (1929); Carol Chillington Rutter, ed., *Documents of the Rose Playhouse* (1984); Tiffany Stern, *Documents of Performance in Early Modern England* (2009); Glynne Wickham, Herbert Berry, and William Ingram, *English Professional Theatre, 1530–1660* (2009).

WILLIAM SHAKESPEARE OF STRATFORD-UPON-AVON, GENTLEMAN

Many people have said that we know very little about William Shakespeare's life – pinheads and postcards are often mentioned as appropriately tiny surfaces on which to record the available information. More imaginatively and perhaps more correctly, Ralph Waldo Emerson wrote, "Shakespeare is the only biographer of Shakespeare. . . . So far from Shakespeare's being the least known, he is the one person in all modern history fully known to us."

In fact, we know more about Shakespeare's life than we do about almost any other English writer's of his era. His last will and testament (dated March 25, 1616) survives, as do numerous legal contracts and court documents involving Shakespeare as principal or witness, and parish records in Stratford and London. Shakespeare appears quite often in official records of King James's royal court, and of course Shakespeare's name appears on numerous title pages and in the written and recorded words of his literary contemporaries Robert Greene, Henry Chettle, Francis Meres, John Davies of Hereford, Ben Jonson, and many others. Indeed, if we make due allowance for the bloating of modern, run-of-the-mill bureaucratic records, more information has survived over the past four hundred years about William Shakespeare of Stratford-upon-Avon, Warwickshire, than is likely to survive in the next four hundred years about any reader of these words.

What we do not have are entire categories of information – Shakespeare's private letters or diaries, drafts and revisions of poems and plays, critical prefaces or essays, commendatory verse for other writers' works, or instructions guiding his fellow actors in their performances, for instance – that we imagine would help us understand and appreciate his surviving writings. For all we know, many such data never existed as written records. Many literary and theatrical critics, not knowing what might once have existed, more or less cheerfully accept the situation; some even make a theoretical virtue of it by claiming that such data are irrelevant to understanding and interpreting the plays and poems.

So, what do we know about William Shakespeare, the man responsible for thirty-seven or perhaps more plays, more than 150 sonnets, two lengthy narrative poems, and some shorter poems?

While many families by the name of Shakespeare (or some variant spelling) can be identified in the English Midlands as far back as the twelfth century, it seems likely that the dramatist's grandfather, Richard, moved to Snitterfield, a town not far from Stratford-upon-Avon, sometime before 1529. In Snitterfield, Richard Shakespeare leased farmland from the very wealthy Robert Arden. By 1552, Richard's son John had moved to a large house on Henley Street in Stratford-upon-Avon, the house that stands today as "The Birthplace." In Stratford, John Shakespeare traded as a glover, dealt in wool, and lent money at interest; he also served in a variety of civic posts, including "High Bailiff," the municipality's equivalent of mayor. In 1557, he married Robert Arden's youngest daughter, Mary. Mary and John had four sons – William was the oldest – and four daughters, of whom only Joan outlived her most celebrated sibling. William was baptized (an event entered in the Stratford parish church records) on April 26, 1564, and it has become customary, without any good factual support, to suppose he was born on April 23, which happens to be the feast day of Saint George, patron saint of England, and is also the date on which Shakespeare died, in 1616. Shakespeare married Anne Hathaway in 1582, when he was eighteen and she was twenty-six; their first child was born five months later. It has been generally assumed that the marriage was enforced and subsequently unhappy, but these are only assumptions; it has been estimated, for instance, that up to one-third of Elizabethan brides were pregnant when they married. Anne and William Shakespeare had three children: Susanna, who married a prominent local physician, John Hall; and the twins Hamnet, who died young in 1596, and Judith, who married Thomas Quiney – apparently a rather shady individual. The name Hamnet was unusual but not unique: he and his twin sister were named for their godparents, Shakespeare's neighbors Hamnet and Judith Sadler. Shakespeare's father died in 1601 (the year of *Hamlet*), and Mary Arden Shakespeare died in 1608 (the year of *Coriolanus*). William Shakespeare's last surviving direct descendant was his granddaughter Elizabeth Hall, who died in 1670.

Between the birth of the twins in 1585 and a clear reference to Shakespeare as a practicing London dramatist in Robert Greene's sensationalizing, satiric pamphlet, *Greene's*

Groatsworth of Wit (1592), there is no record of where William Shakespeare was or what he was doing. These seven so-called lost years have been imaginatively filled by scholars and other students of Shakespeare: some think he traveled to Italy, or fought in the Low Countries, or studied law or medicine, or worked as an apprentice actor/writer, and so on to even more fanciful possibilities. Whatever the biographical facts for those "lost" years, Greene's nasty remarks in 1592 testify to professional envy and to the fact that Shakespeare already had a successful career in London. Speaking to his fellow playwrights, Greene warns both generally and specifically:

> . . . trust them [actors] not: for there is an upstart crow, beautified with our feathers, that with his tiger's heart wrapped in a player's hide supposes he is as well able to bombast out a blank verse as the best of you; and being an absolute Johannes Factotum, is in his own conceit the only Shake-scene in a country.

The passage mimics a line from *3 Henry VI* (hence the play must have been performed before Greene wrote) and seems to say that "Shake-scene" is both actor and playwright, a jack-of-all-trades. That same year, Henry Chettle protested Greene's remarks in *Kind-Heart's Dream,* and each of the next two years saw the publication of poems – *Venus and Adonis* and *Lucrece,* respectively – publicly ascribed to (and dedicated by) Shakespeare. Early in 1595 he was named as one of the senior members of a prominent acting company, the Lord Chamberlain's Men, when they received payment for court performances during the 1594 Christmas season.

Clearly, Shakespeare had achieved both success and reputation in London. In 1596, upon Shakespeare's application, the College of Arms granted his father the now-familiar coat of arms he had taken the first steps to obtain almost twenty years before, and in 1598, John's son – now permitted to call himself "gentleman" – took a 10 percent share in the new Globe playhouse. In 1597, he bought a substantial bourgeois house, called New Place, in Stratford – the garden remains, but Shakespeare's house, several times rebuilt, was torn down in 1759 – and over the next few years Shakespeare spent large sums buying land and making other investments in the town and its environs. Though he worked in London, his family remained in Stratford, and he seems always to have considered Stratford the home he would eventually return to. Something approaching a disinterested appreciation of Shakespeare's popular and professional status appears in Francis Meres's *Palladis Tamia* (1598), a not especially imaginative and perhaps therefore persuasive record of literary reputations. Reviewing contemporary English writers, Meres lists the titles of many of Shakespeare's plays, including one not now known, *Love's Labor's Won*, and praises his "mellifluous & hony-tongued" "sugred Sonnets," which were then circulating in manuscript (they were first collected in 1609). Meres describes Shakespeare as "one of the best" English playwrights of both comedy and tragedy. In *Remains . . . Concerning Britain* (1605), William Camden – a more authoritative source than the imitative Meres – calls Shakespeare one of the "most pregnant witts of these our times" and joins him with such writers as Chapman, Daniel, Jonson, Marston, and Spenser. During the first decades of the seventeenth century, publishers began to attribute numerous play quartos, including some non-Shakespearean ones, to Shakespeare, either by name or initials, and we may assume that they deemed Shakespeare's name and supposed authorship, true or false, commercially attractive.

For the next ten years or so, various records show Shakespeare's dual career as playwright and man of the theater in London, and as an important local figure in Stratford. In 1608–9 his acting company – designated the "King's Men" soon after King James had succeeded Queen Elizabeth in 1603 – rented, refurbished, and opened a small interior playing space, the Blackfriars theater, in London, and Shakespeare was once again listed as a substantial sharer in the group of proprietors of the playhouse. By May 11, 1612, however, he describes himself as a Stratford resident in a London lawsuit – an indication that he had withdrawn from day-to-day professional activity and returned to the town where he had always had his main financial interests. When Shakespeare bought a substantial residential building in London, the Blackfriars Gatehouse, close to the theater of the same name, on March 10, 1613, he is recorded as William Shakespeare "of Stratford upon Avon in the county of Warwick, gentleman," and he named several London residents as the building's trustees. Still, he continued to participate in theatrical activity: when the new Earl of Rutland needed an allegorical design to bear as a shield, or *impresa*, at the celebration of King James's Accession Day, March 24, 1613, the earl's accountant recorded a payment of 44 shillings to Shakespeare for the device with its motto.

For the last few years of his life, Shakespeare evidently concentrated his activities in the town of his birth. Most of the final records concern business transactions in Stratford, ending with the notation of his death on April 23, 1616, and burial in Holy Trinity Church, Stratford-upon-Avon.

The Question of Authorship

The history of ascribing Shakespeare's plays (the poems do not come up so often) to someone else began, as it continues, peculiarly. The earliest published claim that someone else wrote Shakespeare's plays appeared in an 1856 article by Delia Bacon in the American journal *Putnam's Monthly* – although an Englishman, Thomas Wilmot, had shared his doubts in private (even secretive) conversations with friends near the end of the eighteenth century. Bacon's was a sad personal history that ended in madness and poverty, but the year after her article, she published, with great difficulty and the bemused assistance of Nathaniel Hawthorne (then United States Consul in Liverpool, England), her *Philosophy of the Plays of Shakspere Unfolded.* This huge, ornately written, confusing farrago is almost unreadable; sometimes its intents, to say nothing of its arguments, disappear entirely beneath near-raving, ecstatic writing. Tumbled in with much supposed "philosophy" appear the claims that Francis Bacon (from whom Delia Bacon eventually claimed descent), Walter Ralegh, and several other contemporaries of Shakespeare's had written the plays. The book had little impact except as a ridiculed curiosity.

Once proposed, however, the issue gained momentum among people whose conviction was the greater in proportion to their ignorance of sixteenth- and seventeenth-century English literature, history, and society. Another American amateur, Catharine F. Ashmead Windle, made the next influential contribution to the cause when she published *Report to the British Museum* (1882), wherein she promised to open "the Cipher of Francis Bacon," though what she mostly offers, in the words of S. Schoenbaum, is "demented allegorizing." An entire new cottage industry grew from Windle's suggestion that the texts contain hidden, cryptographically discoverable ciphers – "clues" – to their authorship; and today there are not only books devoted to the putative ciphers, but also pamphlets, journals, and newsletters.

Although Baconians have led the pack of those seeking a substitute Shakespeare, in *"Shakespeare" Identified* (1920), J. Thomas Looney became the first published "Oxfordian" when he proposed Edward de Vere, seventeenth earl of Oxford, as the secret author of Shakespeare's plays. Also for Oxford and his "authorship" there are today dedicated societies, articles, journals, and books. Less popular candidates – Queen Elizabeth and Christopher Marlowe among them – have had adherents, but the movement seems to have divided into two main contending factions, Baconian and Oxfordian. (For further details on all the candidates for "Shakespeare," see S. Schoenbaum, *Shakespeare's Lives,* 2nd ed., 1991.)

The Baconians, the Oxfordians, and supporters of other candidates have one trait in common – they are snobs.

Every pro-Bacon or pro-Oxford tract sooner or later claims that the historical William Shakespeare of Stratford-upon-Avon could not have written the plays because he could not have had the training, the university education, the experience, and indeed the imagination or background their author supposedly possessed. Only a learned genius like Bacon or an aristocrat like Oxford could have written such fine plays. (As it happens, lucky male children of the middle class had access to better education than most aristocrats in Elizabethan England – and Oxford was not particularly well educated.) Shakespeare received in the Stratford grammar school a formal education that would daunt many college graduates today; and popular rival playwrights such as the very learned Ben Jonson and George Chapman, both of whom also lacked university training, achieved great artistic success without being taken as Bacon or Oxford.

Besides snobbery, one other quality characterizes the authorship controversy: lack of evidence. A great deal of testimony from Shakespeare's time shows that Shakespeare wrote Shakespeare's plays and that his contemporaries recognized them as distinctive and distinctly superior. (Some of that contemporary evidence is collected in E. K. Chambers, *William Shakespeare: A Study of Facts and Problems,* 2 vols., 1930.) Since that testimony comes from Shakespeare's enemies and theatrical competitors as well as from his coworkers and from the Elizabethan equivalent of literary journalists, it seems unlikely that, if any of these sources had known he was a fraud, they would have failed to record that fact.

Books About Shakespeare's Life

The following books provide scholarly, documented accounts of Shakespeare's life: G. E. Bentley, *Shakespeare: A Biographical Handbook* (1961); E. K. Chambers, *William Shakespeare: A Study of Facts and Problems,* 2 vols. (1930); S. Schoenbaum, *William Shakespeare: A Compact Documentary Life* (1977), and the same author's *Shakespeare's*

The Texts of Shakespeare

As FAR AS WE KNOW, only one manuscript conceivably in Shakespeare's own hand may (and even this is much disputed) exist: a few pages of a play called *Sir Thomas More*, which apparently was never performed. What we do have, as later readers, performers, scholars, students, are printed texts. The earliest of these survive in two forms: quartos and folios. Quartos (from the Latin for "four") are small books, printed on sheets of paper that were then folded twice, to make four leaves or eight pages. When these were bound together, the result was a squarish, eminently portable volume that sold for the relatively small sum of sixpence (translating in modern terms to about $5). In folios, on the other hand, the sheets are folded only once, in half, producing large, impressive volumes taller than they are wide. This was the format for important works of philosophy, science, theology, and literature (the major precedent for a folio Shakespeare was Ben Jonson's *Works*, 1616). The decision to print the works of a popular playwright in folio is an indication of how far up on the social scale the theatrical profession had come during Shakespeare's lifetime. The Shakespeare folio was an expensive book, selling for between fifteen and eighteen shillings, depending on the binding (in modern terms, from about $150 to $180). Twenty Shakespeare plays of the thirty-seven that survive first appeared in quarto, seventeen of which appeared during Shakespeare's lifetime; the rest of the plays are found only in folio.

The First Folio was published in 1623, seven years after Shakespeare's death, and was authorized by his fellow actors, the co-owners of the King's Men. This publication was certainly a mark of the company's enormous respect for Shakespeare; but it was also a way of turning the old plays, most of which were no longer current in the playhouse, into ready money (the folio includes only Shakespeare's plays, not his sonnets or other nondramatic verse). Whatever the motives behind the publication of the folio, the texts it preserves constitute the basis for almost all later editions of the playwright's works. The texts, however, differ from those of the earlier quartos, sometimes in minor respects but often significantly – most strikingly in the two texts of *King Lear*, but also in important ways in *Hamlet, Othello,* and *Troilus and Cressida.* (The variants are recorded in the textual notes to each play.) The differences in these texts represent, in a sense, the essence of theater: the texts of the plays were initially not intended for publication. They were scripts, designed for the actors to perform – the principal life of the play at this period was in performance. And it follows that in Shakespeare's theater the playwright typically had no say either in how his play was performed or in the disposition of his text – he was an employee of the company. The authoritative figures in the theatrical enterprise were the shareholders in the company, who were for the most part the major actors. They decided what plays were to be done; they hired the playwright and often gave him an outline of the play they wanted him to write. Often, too, the play was a collaboration: the company would retain a group of writers and parcel out the scenes among them. The resulting script was then the property of the company, and the actors would revise it as they saw fit during the course of putting it onstage. The resulting text belonged to the company. The playwright had no rights in it once he had been paid. (This system survives largely intact in the movie industry, and most of the playwrights of Shakespeare's time were as anonymous as most screenwriters are today.) The script could also, of course, continue to change as the tastes of audiences and the requirements of the actors changed. Many – perhaps most – plays were revised when they were reintroduced after any substantial absence from the repertory, or when they were performed by a company different from the one that originally commissioned the play.

Shakespeare was an exceptional figure in this world because he was not only a shareholder and actor in his company, but also its leading playwright – he was literally his own boss. He had, moreover, little interest in the publication of his plays, and even those that appeared during his lifetime with the authorization of the company show no signs of any editorial concern on the part of the author. Theater was, for Shakespeare, a fluid and supremely responsive medium – the very opposite of the great classic canonical text that has embodied his works since 1623.

The very fluidity of the original texts, however, has meant that Shakespeare has always had to be edited. Here is an example of how problematic the editorial project inevitably is, a passage from the most famous speech in *Romeo and Juliet,* Juliet's balcony soliloquy beginning "O Romeo, Romeo, wherefore art thou Romeo?" Since the eighteenth century, the standard modern text has read:

> What's Montague? It is nor hand, nor foot,
> Nor arm, nor face, nor any other part
> Belonging to a man. O be some other name!
> What's in a name? That which we call a rose
> By any other name would smell as sweet.
>
> (II.2.40–44)

Editors have three early texts of this play to work from, two quarto texts and the folio. Here is how the First Quarto (1597) reads:

> Whats *Mountague?* It is nor hand nor foote,
> Nor arme, nor face, nor any other part.
> Whats in a name? That which we call a Rose,
> By any other name would smell as sweet:

Here is the Second Quarto (1599):

> Whats *Mountague?* it is nor hand nor foote,
> Nor arme nor face, ô be some other name
> Belonging to a man.
> Whats in a name that which we call a rose,
> By any other word would smell as sweete,

And here is the First Folio (1623):

What's *Mountague* ? it is nor hand nor foote,
Nor arme, nor face, O be some other name
Belonging to a man.
What ? in a names that which we call a Rose,
By any other word would smell as sweete,

There is in fact no early text that reads as our modern text does – and this is the most famous speech in the play. Instead, we have three quite different texts, all of which are clearly some version of the same speech, but none of which seems to us a final or satisfactory version. The transcendently beautiful passage in modern editions is an editorial invention: editors have succeeded in conflating and revising the three versions into something we recognize as great poetry. Is this what Shakespeare "really" wrote? Who can say? What we can say is that Shakespeare always had performance, not a book, in mind.

Books About the Shakespeare Texts

The standard studies of the printing history of the First Folio are W. W. Greg, *The Shakespeare First Folio* (1955), and Charlton Hinman, *The Printing and Proof-Reading of the First Folio of Shakespeare* (1963). J. K. Walton, *The Quarto Copy for the First Folio of Shakespeare* (1971), is a useful survey of the relation of the quartos to the folio. The second edition of Charlton Hinman's *Norton Facsimile* of the First Folio (1996), with a new introduction by Peter Blayney, is indispensable. Stanley Wells, Gary Taylor, John Jowett, and William Montgomery, *William Shakespeare: A Textual Companion,* keyed to the Oxford text, gives a comprehensive survey of the editorial situation for all the plays and poems.

Introduction

THERE ARE ONLY two famous hunchbacks in Western literature: Shakespeare's Richard and Victor Hugo's Quasimodo. Hugo's sympathetic portrait teeters on the edge of sentimentality. His hunchback, kindly and loving but unloved and lonely, trapped in Notre Dame with only the bells for friends, a perennial failure, is at the opposite pole from the brutally comic and terrifyingly diabolic evil of Richard, Duke of Gloucester, the essence of unstoppable ambition. They share their isolation and their stifling awareness of their deformity but little else. Both know that the world does not understand them but where Quasimodo is forced into withdrawal, away from the crowded streets of Paris, Richard has, as he wishes, "the world to bustle in" (I.1.152).

If the citizens of Hugo's medieval Paris should have treated Quasimodo with greater humane understanding, many of the inhabitants of Shakespeare's medieval England know only too well the horrific malevolence of the figure they are dealing with and yet are still unable to do anything about his evil "plots" and "inductions dangerous" (I.1.32). As Queen Margaret tells Richard's mother, in the most appalling image of childbirth I know,

> From forth the kennel of thy womb hath crept
> A hellhound that doth hunt us all to death:
> That dog, that had his teeth before his eyes, . . .
> Thy womb let loose to chase us to our graves.
> (IV.4.47–49, 54)

Apparently impotent in the face of Richard's actions, Richard's victims share the knowledge of their fate, "lambs" (50) in Richard's slaughterhouse.

To a considerable extent, Shakespeare found his Richard ready-formed – or, rather, already deformed – in sources familiar to him, the chronicles of English history like Edward Hall's *The Union of the Two Noble and Illustre Families of Lancaster and York* (published in 1548) or Raphael Holinshed's *The Chronicles of England, Scotland and Ireland* (first published in 1577, revised and expanded in 1587). These and the other chronicles Shakespeare might have consulted offered a Richard who was strikingly unlike any other figure in their immense and detailed accounts of historical events. Their source for Richard, incorporated directly into their narratives, was Sir Thomas More's exhilarating and intensely dramatic creation of Richard as the demonized epitome of evil in his *History of King Richard III* (first published in English in 1557 and in Latin in 1566). More's account may be history as purposive propaganda but it also reads as an exciting story, turning the historian into a narrator with a sense of drama as acute as Richard himself, a narrator who creates (or records) scenes so packed with direct speech that they barely needed dramatizing. Shakespeare had read the "tragedies" of many of his characters (Clarence, Buckingham, Hastings, and others) in the mostly dull poetry of *A Mirror for Magistrates* (published in 1559 but often revised and expanded thereafter), a collection of highly moral views of the consequences of the political ethics of various figures of English history. But *A Mirror* is most likely to have functioned as a warning of how not to make good poetic fiction out of history. More's biography of Richard, even in its diluted form in Hall or Holinshed, showed that Richard's life was history already teetering on the brink of drama.

Shakespeare's own version of Richard does not begin with this play. If now we most often encounter *Richard III*, whether read or watched on stage and film, as a play on its own, Shakespeare conceived of the play's narrative and the central character emerging from the conflicts and torments of a country riven by civil war, a sequence that he had already charted at unprecedented theatrical length. An audience watching *Richard III* apart from the other plays in the group of four history plays now called the "first tetralogy" can make little sense of the names invoked in Margaret's litany of loss:

> I had an Edward, till a Richard killed him;
> I had a husband, till a Richard killed him:
> Thou hadst an Edward, till a Richard killed him;
> Thou hadst a Richard, till a Richard killed him.
>   (IV.4.40–43)

But heard at the end of the group, with these deaths as they had been dramatized in the three parts of *King Henry VI* fresh in the spectators' minds, the catalogue is an unbearable summoning-up of those memories for audience and lamenting women alike. The characters have a theatrical history as well as one in the chronicles.

"Crookback Richard," as the 1594 First Quarto edition of *Henry VI, Part 2* called him in the stage direction for his very first entrance (V.1.119 s.d.), had been the plays' usual instrument of murder. The *Henry VI* plays are full of insults traded between rival factions, but Richard had brought to this repeated ritual a particular brand of acerbic wit, attracting in response a recurrent mocking of his deformity: a "foul indigested lump" to Clifford (*Henry VI, Part 2*, V.1.155) and "an indigested and deformèd lump" to King Henry VI just before Richard murders him (*Henry VI, Part 3*, V.6.51). Nothing had prepared the audience for Richard's sudden, unprecedented outburst at the midpoint of *Henry VI, Part 3*. Soliloquies are not common in these plays; the most striking had been the one by Richard's father, Duke of York, outlining his plans to take power (*Henry VI, Part 2*, III.1.331–83). But where Richard, Duke of York, had spoken to himself ("Now, York, or never, steel thy fearful thoughts," line 331) or warningly to the nobles who had left him with an army, Richard, Duke of Gloucester, sets out his special brand of colossal ambition in a colossal speech of more than 70 lines spoken directly to the audience (*Henry VI, Part 3,* III.2.124–95). It was always clear that York had had his sights set on the crown but there had not been the slightest clue of Richard's desire.

At this point, Richard's yearning appears like a deliberate compensation for the exclusion from love consequent on deformity:

> And am I then a man to be beloved?
> O, monstrous fault, to harbor such a thought!
> Then, since this earth affords no joy to me
> But to command, . . .
> I'll make my heaven to dream upon the crown.
> (*Henry VI, Part 3,* III.2.163–68)

But the unfulfilled desire is also an agony, and murder is one method for release from that tormenting pain:

> I . . . [t]orment myself to catch the English crown.
> And from that torment I will free myself,
> Or hew my way out with a bloody ax.
>
> (174–81)

So far Richard could be outlining a comprehensible psychological self-image, a description of motivation that sees the deformity at birth as the straightforward and adequate source for the embittered man. But Richard moves on to identify himself as, above all else, a supreme performer: "Why, I can smile, and murder whiles I smile" (182). With such confidence in his own virtuosity and with such a clear view of the means to achieve his aims, Richard ends his speech as the actors' actor, the man for whom the world is an almost comically easy space in which to work:

> I can add colors to the chameleon,
> Change shapes with Proteus for advantages,

And set the murderous Machiavel to school.
Can I do this, and cannot get a crown?
Tut, were it farther off, I'll pluck it down.
(191–95)

This fluidly metamorphic Protean shape changer will be frequently defined by others in *Richard III* as animal, as if the unformed lump could as easily have become something disturbingly other than human. Margaret labels him a dog at his birth but she also calls him "hog" (I.3.228) from his coat of arms, "bottled spider," and "bunch-backed toad" (242, 246). Lurking further behind this tension between Richard as deformed human and Richard as animal lies a larger inhumanity, the threat of Richard as devil or at least as the figure of Vice, the temptingly enticing image of nonhuman viciousness familiar to audiences from a range of earlier drama.

If actors revel in the theatricality, the performative brilliance of Richard himself as well as Shakespeare's writing of the role, they also have to confront the physical difficulty of the role, its twisted shape placing an immense strain on the actor's body, given the high proportion of the play in which Richard is onstage, for Richard is second only to Hamlet as the longest role in Shakespeare. Anthony Sher (Royal Shakespeare Company, 1984) used crutches to create the image of Richard as spider scuttling over the stage but he also used two different hunchbacks, one for each shoulder, so that the strain of repeated performances was not always putting the same distorting pressure on his spine. Simon Russell Beale (Royal Shakespeare Company, 1992), visually the "bunch-backed toad," had to withdraw from the role for surgery to his back. Only Ian McKellen (Royal National Theatre, 1990, and on film, 1996), by reducing the emphasis on deformity, solved the physical problem of performance.

But the physical problems are ones actors willingly confront, for Richard, like Hamlet, establishes a peculiarly close contact with the theater audience, an engagement actors relish. Throughout the early scenes of *Richard III*, Richard establishes a relationship with the audience that is so wittily charming that it becomes almost impossible for the spectators to maintain their moral integrity. Caught by Richard as much as his onstage victims, we find the invocation of moral dismay itself almost comical as if we are being pompous in harboring any reluctance to accept Richard's right to manipulate language and murder people, both as he pleases. Sustained verbal dexterity replaces physical beauty as a means of his winning Anne, whose husband and father-in-law Richard has murdered. A hint of a prophecy in the ear of his brother, King Edward IV, enables Richard to have his other brother, Clarence, arrested. A single hesitant word, "If" (III.4.74), is enough for Richard to demand Hastings' head. Richard's rise ought to be terrifying in its irresistibility but it is both comical in its demonstration of his control over others' weakness and diabolically engaging.

But in Shakespeare's treatment of Richard as king, rather than of the Richard who makes his way to the crown, the earlier Richard is thrown into sharp relief. Most actors playing Richard and most audiences watching productions find that the play's dynamic alters irrevocably once Richard enters crowned as king in IV.2. Such wit as he has left to him has nothing of the earlier verve, its linguistic play tired and charmless:

DERBY   Richmond is on the seas.
KING RICHARD
There let him sink, and be the seas on him!
                          (IV.4.462–63)

The figure whose power in the world was both emblematized and embodied in his power over language itself now seems as mundanely caught by the conventions of language as his victims had been. Richard's control over the characters and hence their actions also vanishes. The long wooing of Queen Elizabeth to make a match with her daughter (IV.4.199–430), so clearly a mirroring of the wooing of Anne early in the play that it has often been cut onstage, having been mistaken for needless repetition, shows Richard for the first time completely misunderstanding the outcome of an encounter, reading as success something that is much more ambivalent. He may assume that she is a "Relenting fool, and shallow, changing woman" (431) but the next news we have of her is that her daughter has married Richmond instead.

The apparent victory over her objections is itself accomplished not through establishing a superiority in intelligence in meeting her complaints culminating in placing his life in her hands, as he had so brilliantly done with Anne, but through a terrifying threat of universal destruction:

> Without her, follows to myself and thee,
> Herself, the land, and many a Christian soul,
> Death, desolation, ruin, and decay.
> It cannot be avoided but by this;
> It will not be avoided but by this.
>
> (407–11)

Anne's capitulation had been transparent to Richard and audience alike, but the actions of Elizabeth can be differently read by Richard and the audience, Richard's assumption of her agreement being rejected by the audience's perception of her double meaning: "you shall understand from me her mind" (429). This moment establishes an unprecedented fracture between Richard and the audience, his natural ally. He may continue to talk directly to the audience from time to time – though far less frequently than earlier – but his expectation of our complicity may no longer be reciprocated.

The gap that begins now to open up reaches its next stage in Richard's soliloquy after the ghosts have cursed him (V.3.178–207). Where cursing had earlier been the especial prerogative of Margaret, a living ghost, it now becomes the practice of the parade of Richard's victims. Richard's response on waking is to speak in a way that is not only new to him but new to Shakespeare and to English drama. The verse lines break up into numerous tiny sentences. There is a horror and urgency, a hesitancy and insecurity that has never before been part of Richard's voice; Shakespeare has found a remarkable and energizing new style in which to represent an extreme state of emotion.

Though earlier Richard had buttonholed us, chatted to us easily and confidently, he now finds himself in dialogue with himself. Soliloquy is often understood to mean speaking with oneself rather than speaking by oneself, but Richard's soliloquies have been a dialogue with us. Now "There's none else by" (183). The multiple voices with which Richard has to negotiate, the "thousand several tongues" (194), come from his conscience, from within him, rather than from outside, from the others who object to his actions and who have been his victims. As he confronts these voices, debating with himself, he finds that the notion of self begins itself to change: "Richard loves Richard; that is, I and I" (184). The line seems simple enough but the tendency of editors, from the printers of the Second Quarto onwards, to emend the last phrase to "I am I" suggests how complex the thought is. The emendation creates unity: to say Richard loves Richard is to recognize that one loves oneself. The form first published, "I and I," creates two selves, a Richard who loves someone else. Richard's overpowering ego, so overpowering that it has for so long controlled the audience as well as the other characters, has now subdivided, and the resultant selves, constricted within the action rather than able to engage in easy conversation with us outside it, seem distinctly lessened. Where Marlowe's Tamburlaine the Great (c. 1588), whose ambition had been to conquer the world, dies with the frustrating awareness, as he looks at a map, "And shall I die, and this unconquerèd," Richard's diminution in the last scenes is the literally self-destructive peril of achieving one's ambition.

Shakespeare's charting of Richard was his most extraordinary achievement in characterization to date but the depiction of the opposition to Richard is markedly less surely handled. Tyrrel's set-piece account of the murder of the princes in the Tower (IV.3.1–22) ought to convince us that it was indeed a "tyrannous and bloody act." His description of the hesitancy of Dighton and Forrest, placed to balance the conscience-stricken hesitancy of the First Murderer of Clarence, invokes a lyric style that is dramatically ineffective:

> Their lips were four red roses on a stalk,
> And in their summer beauty kissed each other.
> (12–13)

The murder of children as the culminating deed of tyranny, a device Shakespeare would return to in *Macbeth*, is intellectually damnable but the language does not have the emotional impact for which it seems to be striving. A similar problem is present in Clarence's dream (I.4.1–63), an example of virtuoso set-piece description far more successful as dramatic language than Tyrrel's speech. It functions as premonition of Richard's actions and invocation of the conscience that Richard himself will lack until virtually the end of the play, and yet its very length and its ornateness as dream-narrative serve to suspend the action of the play, working against the narrative drive Richard has initiated.

Indeed, for much of its length, *Richard III* displays a careful formality of dramatic language that typifies early Shakespeare. Even though Richard can be sharply aware of the maneuvers of his own language (as when he says to Lady Anne, "To leave this keen encounter of our wits / And fall something into a slower method –" I.2.115–16), the strong end-stopping and visibility of rhetorical tropes serve to create a verse style far less swiftly effective in its dramatic verve than Shakespeare would later achieve, making this long play seem far longer than, say, *Hamlet*. Yet played at something approaching full length, as the play hardly ever is in the theater, *Richard III* shows Shakespeare's new skills in managing to control the dramatic processing of historical narrative and its consequentially large cast of characters.

If Richard's rise is a triumph of individual will, then this concern with the self also marks most of his victims. In the depiction of a state exhausted by the long series of conflicts that Shakespeare had charted in the sequence thus far, *Richard III* seems full of people desperate to rise above or at least to survive the chaos of factions and realignments in which they exist. Richard is hardly the play's only example of egocentric ambition. Buckingham, in particular, in his intelligent understanding of the means to manipulate and scheme, shows himself entirely Richard's equal except for the latter's unmatchable diabolism and charm. Hastings' speech before execution is strikingly an exception both in his awareness of his own stupidity and, more significantly, in his selfless concern for the consequences of Richard's rise for the country as well as himself:

> Woe, woe for England, not a whit for me,
> For I, too fond, might have prevented this.
> (III.4.80–81)

In Queen Margaret, however, Shakespeare established not only a resistant character but also a structure of denial of Richard's dominance. When Laurence Olivier eliminated Margaret from his film of *Richard III* (1955), as Ian McKellen would do in his adaptation for Richard Loncraine in 1996, he was, as in so many other details, simply following a strong and long-lived theatrical tradition. Margaret can appear in production as nothing more than a haunting presence, a voice of the preceding plays, a brutal reminder to the play's people of their history already accomplished. But her recurrent cursing also functions as a form of prophetic utterance, predicting the fate of the court. As Rivers, Grey, and Vaughan face death they cannot help but remember Margaret: "Now Margaret's curse

is fall'n upon our heads" (III.3.15). Hastings in III.4 and
Buckingham in V.1, using similar words, also remind
themselves – and, in so doing, of course remind the
audience – of the accurate outcome of Margaret's "heavy"
curse, underlining the connections across the play. Margaret's entrance in I.3 has the remarkable effect of recon-
ciling the factions of the court in their opposition to her
with far greater unity than the king's attempts at peace-
making. Each had been able to dismiss her words as the
ravings of a madwoman:

> RICHARD
> What doth she say, my Lord of Buckingham?
> BUCKINGHAM
> Nothing that I respect, my gracious lord.
>   (I.3.295–96)

But they come to recognize the truth of her statement:
"Margaret was a prophetess" (I.3.301 – compare Buckingham's memory of the line at V.1.27).

Prophecy always occupies a peculiar place in drama; for
one thing it is much more likely to be accurate than in
other contexts. It functions as a form of dramatic structure, a built-in expectation of its likely fulfillment. Margaret's predictions shape the play's form, anticipating both
Richard's success in dealing with all who stand in his way
to the throne and his eventual failure. She is aligned with
the play's other prophets, like the "bard of Ireland" who
told Richard that he would "not live long after [he] saw
Richmond" (IV.2.104–6). As the repository of the play's
longest vision of the historical past and the accurate vision
of a historical future, Margaret offers a structuring voice, a
prediction of historical and therefore dramatic event within
which Richard's actions are contained.

Individual action, even the extreme of virtuosic control
that Richard manifests, takes its place, through Margaret's
utterances, within a larger schema, one over which individuals have no control and which might be seen as

providentially ordered, a system that might prove to manifest the divine will. If the recurrent laments in the play point to an anxiety over divine inaction remedied by Richard's eventual defeat, then Richmond's accession as Henry VII points to an equally anxious need for divine reassurance in a series of tentative requests. "And let their heirs – God, if thy will be so – / Enrich the time to come with smooth-faced peace" (V.5.32–33) is a sentiment whose circularity to the play's opening vision of peace is not entirely comforting, even though the time for "caper[ing] nimbly in a lady's chamber" (I.1.12) has changed into a time for securing the future of the kingdom through producing heirs, especially at the end of a play in which a number of potential heirs to the throne have been murdered and in which the legitimacy of individuals' rights of succession has been repeatedly questioned. Peace itself is still seen as intensely fragile, desperately needing God's approval to survive:

> Now civil wounds are stopped, peace lives again:
> That she may long live here, God say amen.
>
> (V.5.40–41)

That final prayer, a concern for a national peace rather than individual triumph, epitomizes the extent to which Richard's rise had denied the concerns of nation and national history. Richard at times seems almost to escape the limits of historical discourse, to be beating at the boundaries of the historiographic narrative that controls him. He is able to invoke a concept of nation, as when his oration to his army before the climactic battle is built around the otherness, the non-Englishness of Richmond's Breton troops (V.3.315–42), as he encourages his "gentlemen of England" (339), while Richmond's rousing speech focuses on the need to defeat a single enemy, Richard himself (238–71), calling on God and England's patron saint: "God and Saint George!" (271). But Richard is a character beyond the constraints of nation.

When, in *Macbeth*, Macduff enters with the tyrant's head and announces, "The time is free" (V.8.55), he suggests that more than Scotland has been liberated by this act: history itself begins again or at least afresh with this moment. The death of Richard III seems to have a similar potency, for his dramatic power so often breaks out of the stage that he can seem to threaten history. On film, Ian McKellen's Richard, embedded in an alternative history of a pro-fascist England in the 1920s and 1930s, showed a tamer monster than Olivier's, whose terrifying mania explored to the full the play's toying with melodramatic excesses. For Richard is a fantasticated imagining of evil that serves to justify the final settlement of the civil wars Shakespeare had documented in the cycle of four plays into the country's exhausted reordering under Richmond. It is as if Richard's absolute individualism is the grotesquely logical product of the sustained faction-driven conflicts of the past. In this tension between the workings of history and its denial, between individual ambition and structured – perhaps divinely providential – control, Richard is the circumscribed denial of time.

The rise of Richard, Duke of Gloucester, and the defeat of King Richard III become, for Shakespeare, historical necessities, and the drama is a way of making sense of history, of finding a larger and perhaps a comforting meaning in the chronicles. In 1941 for Bertolt Brecht, trying to dramatize the rise of Adolf Hitler and the culpability of those who had failed to oppose him, in the play that would eventually become *The Resistible Rise of Arturo Ui*, it seemed only natural to write a play strikingly like Shakespeare's *Richard III*. For both Brecht and Shakespeare, it is the fullest confrontation with evil in its most temptingly and comically immoral form that is the enormous moral obligation placed on the writer who seeks to dramatize the tragic potentials of history.

PETER HOLLAND
The Shakespeare Institute,
The University of Birmingham

Note on the Text

To put it mildly, the textual history of the early editions of *Richard III* is complicated. Scholars continue to argue about the precise status of each text, the source of the copy for it, and the implications of its textual evidence. The play was first printed in 1597 in a quarto edition (Q). There were seven further quarto editions, in 1598, 1602, 1605, 1612, 1622, 1629, and 1634. None of these later quartos has any independent authority. The play was printed in the First Folio (F), the first collected edition of Shakespeare's plays, in 1623. Thus much for the agreed basic facts.

How precisely the copy for Q was created is a matter of intense debate, and this note offers the briefest of summaries of the current state of textual play. Long argued to be a memorial reconstruction by certain of the actors, perhaps when the company was out on tour, Q bears so few traces of other comparable cases of "bad" quartos that it is really in a class of its own. It cuts a number of wordy passages present in F, exactly the kinds of passages often cut in the play's long stage history. It differs in hundreds of individual readings where it may be better or worse than F but is most significant just for being different. It would seem to be a text that reflects performance and that shows a sure hand of revision by a playwright. Occasionally it seems to differ from F in ways that suggest a wish for the play to stand more comfortably independent of the rest of the tetralogy.

For a number of reasons, recent textual scholarship tends to argue that the text of F certainly represents the play at an earlier stage of development than that represented by Q. It is agreed that F was set partly from a copy of Q3 and partly from a copy of Q6, both corrected by reference to an independent manuscript, which has some authorial significance but which was probably not in Shakespeare's hand. Precisely which passages were set from Q3 and which from Q6 is still a matter of debate. Two sections of F (III.1.1–158 and from V.3.48 to the end of the play) seem not to have been corrected against the independent manuscript.

The text of this edition follows F except for those two passages for which it has no independent authority; for these, Q provides copy. There are also a small number of lines that are not present in F and that are taken from Q; the only substantial such section is IV.2.97–115, Richard's ignoring Buckingham's requests. Readers should remember that such Q-only passages were almost certainly never intended to coexist in a text with other passages that survive only in F and which Q therefore probably cut deliberately. F is divided into acts and scenes, but this has been corrected by editors since 1709. I have kept to the traditional scene divisions even where they glide over a clear stage (see commentary in Act V in particular).

The collations below list departures from F (except for the two passages where they list departures from Q) and the source of the reading of this edition. F2 is the Second Folio (1632). "Eds" stands for emendation by editors from Rowe in 1709 onwards. There is no attempt to record all passages where Q differs from F; such documentation is well beyond the scope of this edition, and it is extremely difficult for readers to reconstruct Q from such lists. Anyone interested in such problems should consult quarto and folio facsimiles.

The adopted reading in this edition appears in italics.

I.1 41 s.d. *Clarence guarded* (eds) Clarence with a gard of men (Q) Clarence, and Brakenbury, guarded (F) 45 *the* th' 52 *for* but 75 *his* her 133 *prey* play
I.2 39 *stand* Stand'st 78 *a* (not in F) 80 *t' accuse* (eds) to curse (Q, F) 126 *rend* rent 201 RICHARD (not in F) 202 *To . . . give* (not in F) 225 *Sirs . . . corpse* (not in F)

I.3 17 *come the lords* comes the Lord 68–69 *he . . . it* (eds; 69 *[Of . . . it]*
not in F) thereby he may gather / The ground of your ill will and to
remove it (Q) 114 *Tell . . . said* (not in F) 155 *Ah* (eds) A 309 QUEEN
ELIZABETH (eds) Qu. (Q) Hast. (Q6) Mar. (F) 321 *you* yours; *lords* (Q
Lo.) lord 342, 350 FIRST MURDERER (eds) Execu. (Q) Vil. (F) 355 BOTH
MURDERERS (eds) Vil. (F; speech not in Q)

I.4 58 *methoughts* me thought 100 *I* we 121 *Faith* (not in F) 125 *Zounds*
Come 146 *Zounds* (not in F) 174 BOTH (eds) Am. (Q) 2 (F) 186 *death?*
(F2) death, 187 *law,* (F2) law? 189–90 *to have . . . sins* for any good-
nesse (F) 226 *O, if you* If you do 237 *And . . . other* (not in F) 266
As . . . distress (after l. 260 in F; not in Q) 275 *heavens* Heaven

II.1 s.d. *Flourish . . . Buckingham* (F adds "Woodvill," repeating "Rivers") 5 *in* to 7 *Hastings and Rivers* (eds) Rivers and Hastings (Q) Dorset and Rivers (F) 39 *God* heaven 57 *unwittingly* unwillingly 59 *By*
To 68 *That . . . me* (F follows with "Of you Lord Woodvill, and Lord
Scales of you": both names are titles of Rivers, who has already been
referred to in l. 67) 70 *Englishman* Englishmen 93 *but* and 108 *at* and

II.2 1 BOY Edw. 3 GIRL (eds) Daugh. (F throughout) Boy (Q) 47 *I* (not in
F) 83 *weep* weepes 84–85 *and . . . weep* (not in F) 142, 154 *Ludlow*
London 145 *With . . . hearts* (not in F); QUEEN ELIZABETH, DUCHESS OF
YORK (eds) Ans. (Q)

II.3 43 *Ensuing* Pursuing (catchword in F: "Ensuing")

II.4 1 *hear* heard 21 ARCHBISHOP (eds) Car. (Q) Yor. (F) 65 *death* earth

III.1 150 s.d. *Hastings* (eds) Hast. Dors. (Q)

III.2 3 s.d. *Enter Lord Hastings* (as F, but F places after l. 5) 78 *you do* (not
in F) 91 *talked* talke

III.3 1 *Come . . . prisoners* (not in F)

III.4 58 *I . . . say* (not in F) 82 *raze* rowse 83 *But* And

III.5 18 s.d. *Enter . . . head* (as in F, but F places after l. 20) 20 *innocence*
Innocencie 66 *cause* case 104 *Penker* (eds) Peuker

III.7 20 *mine* my; *to an* toward 40 *wisdoms* wisdome 43 *No . . . lord* (not
in F) 83 *My lord* (not in F) 125 *her* his 126 *Her* His 127 *Her* (eds) His
(F; line omitted in Q) 219 *Zounds, I'll* we will 220 *O . . . Buckingham*
(not in F) 247 *cousin* Cousins

IV.2 13 *liege* Lord 70 *there* then 88 *Hereford* Hertford 96–114 *perhaps –* [l. 96, second time] *. . . today* (not in F)

IV.3 5 *ruthless* ruthfull 15 *once* one 31 *at* and 53 *leads* leds

IV.4 10 *unblown* unblowed 39 *Tell . . . mine* (not in F) 45 *holp'st* (Q3)
hopst (Q, F) 52 *That excellent . . . earth* (as in F, but follows l. 53) 64
Thy The 112 *weary* wearied 118 *nights . . . days* night . . . day 128
intestate intestine 141 *Where* Where't 239 *or* and 268 *Would I* I
would 274 *sometimes* sometime 284 *is* (not in F) 323 *loan* (eds)
loue 324 *Often times* (eds) Often-times 365 *Harp on . . . break* (as Q;
follows l. 363 in F) 369 *holy* lordly 377 *God – / God's* Heaven. / Hea-
nens 392 *in* with 396 *o'erpast* repast 417 *peevish-fond* (eds) peevish,
fond (Q) peevish found (F) 431 s.d. *Enter Ratcliffe* (as in Q, which
omits l. 432; F places after l. 432) 444 *Ratcliffe* (eds) Catesby 490 *Ay,
ay* I 534 *tidings* Newes

V.3 28 *you* (F2) your 50 *What . . .* (From this point to the end of the play,

F has no independent authority; notes therefore only list departures from Q.) **59** CATESBY (eds) Rat. **80** *sit* (Q2) set **101** *sundered* (Q3) sundried **132** *sit* (Q2) set **146** *Will* (Q2) Wel **151 s.d.** *Enter . . . young Princes* (In Q the ghosts of the two princes precede the ghost of Hastings; in Q3 the order is that of the sequence of their deaths.) **271 s.d.** *Ratcliffe [, and Soldiers]* (eds) Rat, &c. **283** *not* (Q2) nor **302** *boot* (Q3) bootes **326** *milksop* (Q6) milkesopt

V.5 13 DERBY (F; not in Q)

The Tragedy of
King Richard the Third

[NAMES OF THE ACTORS

KING EDWARD IV
DUCHESS OF YORK, *his mother*
EDWARD, PRINCE OF WALES *(later Edward V)*⎫
RICHARD, DUKE OF YORK   ⎬ *his sons*
GEORGE, DUKE OF CLARENCE ⎫
RICHARD, DUKE OF GLOUCESTER ⎬ *his brothers*
  (later Richard III)
CLARENCE'S SON
CLARENCE'S DAUGHTER

QUEEN ELIZABETH, *wife of Edward IV*
ANTHONY WOODEVILLE, EARL RIVERS, *her brother*
MARQUESS OF DORSET ⎫
LORD GREY   ⎬ *her sons*
SIR THOMAS VAUGHAN

GHOST OF KING HENRY VI
QUEEN MARGARET, *widow of Henry VI*
GHOST OF PRINCE EDWARD, *his son*
LADY ANNE, *Prince Edward's widow*

WILLIAM, LORD HASTINGS, *Lord Chamberlain*
LORD STANLEY, EARL OF DERBY
HENRY, EARL OF RICHMOND *(later Henry VII,*
  son-in-law to Stanley)
EARL OF OXFORD ⎫
SIR JAMES BLUNT ⎬ *followers of Richmond*
SIR WALTER HERBERT⎭

DUKE OF BUCKINGHAM
DUKE OF NORFOLK
SIR RICHARD RATCLIFFE
SIR WILLIAM CATESBY   *followers of Richard,*
SIR JAMES TYRREL   *Duke of Gloucester*
TWO MURDERERS
A PAGE

CARDINAL BOURCHIER, *Archbishop of Canterbury*
ARCHBISHOP OF YORK
BISHOP OF ELY
JOHN, *a priest*
CHRISTOPHER URSWICK, *a priest*

SIR ROBERT BRAKENBURY, *Lieutenant of*
   the Tower of London
LORD MAYOR OF LONDON
A SCRIVENER
HASTINGS, *a pursuivant*
SHERIFF
TRESSEL AND BERKELEY, *gentlemen attending Lady Anne*
LORDS, BISHOPS, ALDERMEN, CITIZENS, ATTENDANTS,
MESSENGERS, SOLDIERS

SCENE: *England*]
*

The Tragedy of
King Richard the Third

∾ I.1 *Enter Richard Duke of Gloucester solus.*

RICHARD
Now is the winter of our discontent
Made glorious summer by this son of York;   2
And all the clouds that lowered upon our house
In the deep bosom of the ocean buried.
Now are our brows bound with victorious wreaths,
Our bruisèd arms hung up for monuments,   6
Our stern alarums changed to merry meetings,   7
Our dreadful marches to delightful measures.   8
Grim-visaged war hath smoothed his wrinkled front,   9
And now, instead of mounting barbèd steeds   10
To fright the souls of fearful adversaries,   11
He capers nimbly in a lady's chamber   12
To the lascivious pleasing of a lute.   13
But I, that am not shaped for sportive tricks   14
Nor made to court an amorous looking glass,
I, that am rudely stamped, and want love's majesty   16
To strut before a wanton ambling nymph,   17

I.1 A London street **s.d.** *solus* alone **2** *son of York* Edward IV, son of Richard, Duke of York (punning on the sun in Edward's emblem) **6** *arms* armor; *monuments* memorials **7** *alarums* calls to arms **8** *measures* stately dances **9** *front* forehead **10** *barbèd* armed with protective covering, studded or spiked, on breast and flanks **11** *fearful* timid **12** *capers* leaps in a dance **13** *lascivious pleasing* seductive charm **14** *sportive* amorous **16** *rudely stamped* coarsely shaped (as in minting a coin) **17** *ambling* strolling

18   I, that am curtailed of this fair proportion,
19   Cheated of feature by dissembling Nature,
20   Deformed, unfinished, sent before my time
    Into this breathing world, scarce half made up,
22   And that so lamely and unfashionable
23   That dogs bark at me as I halt by them –
24   Why, I, in this weak piping time of peace,
    Have no delight to pass away the time,
    Unless to see my shadow in the sun
27   And descant on mine own deformity.
    And therefore, since I cannot prove a lover
    To entertain these fair well-spoken days,
30   I am determinèd to prove a villain
    And hate the idle pleasures of these days.
32   Plots have I laid, inductions dangerous,
33   By drunken prophecies, libels, and dreams,
34   To set my brother Clarence and the king
    In deadly hate the one against the other;
    And if King Edward be as true and just
    As I am subtle, false, and treacherous,
38   This day should Clarence closely be mewed up
    About a prophecy which says that G
40   Of Edward's heirs the murderer shall be.
    Dive, thoughts, down to my soul – here Clarence
      comes!
      Enter Clarence guarded, and Brakenbury.
    Brother, good day. What means this armèd guard
    That waits upon your grace?
CLARENCE   His majesty,

---

18 *proportion* shape 19 *feature* appearance; *dissembling* deceiving (because my greatness is cloaked by a false appearance) 22 *unfashionable* misshapen 23 *halt* limp 24 *piping* (the pipe or recorder was associated with peace, as the fife with war) 27 *descant* discourse, compose variations on a simple theme (the speech illustrates this line: the theme, Richard's deformity) 32 *inductions* initial plans 33 *drunken prophecies* prophecies uttered under the influence of drink 34 *Clarence* (Edward IV, George, Duke of Clarence, and Richard, Duke of Gloucester, were brothers) 38 *mewed up* caged (like a hawk)

Tend'ring my person's safety, hath appointed   44
This conduct to convey me to the Tower.   45

RICHARD
Upon what cause?

CLARENCE   Because my name is George.

RICHARD
Alack, my lord, that fault is none of yours:
He should for that commit your godfathers.   48
O, belike his majesty hath some intent   49
That you should be new-christened in the Tower.   50
But what's the matter, Clarence, may I know?

CLARENCE
Yea, Richard, when I know; for I protest
As yet I do not. But, as I can learn,
He hearkens after prophecies and dreams,
And from the crossrow plucks the letter G,   55
And says a wizard told him that by G   56
His issue disinherited should be.
And for my name of George begins with G,
It follows in his thought that I am he.
These, as I learn, and suchlike toys as these   60
Hath moved his highness to commit me now.   61

RICHARD
Why, this it is, when men are ruled by women:
'Tis not the king that sends you to the Tower;
My Lady Grey his wife, Clarence, 'tis she   64
That tempts him to this harsh extremity.
Was it not she, and that good man of worship,
Anthony Woodeville, her brother there,   67
That made him send Lord Hastings to the Tower,
From whence this present day he is delivered?

---

44 *Tend'ring* being concerned for (irony) 45 *conduct* escort; *convey* conduct (with play on "steal"); *Tower* the Tower of London (frequently used as a prison) 48 *godfathers* (who named a child at baptism) 49 *belike* probably 50 *new-christened* (anticipates, ironically, Clarence's drowning in I.4) 55 *crossrow* alphabet 56 *wizard* wise man or male witch 60 *toys* trifles, fancies 61 *commit* arrest 64 *Lady Grey* Edward IV's wife, Elizabeth, widow of Sir John Grey 67 *Woodeville* i.e., Earl Rivers (trisyllabic)

70   We are not safe, Clarence, we are not safe.

CLARENCE

       By heaven, I think there is no man secure
72   But the queen's kindred, and night-walking heralds
73   That trudge betwixt the king and Mistress Shore.
       Heard you not what an humble suppliant
       Lord Hastings was for his delivery?

RICHARD

76   Humbly complaining to her deity
77   Got my Lord Chamberlain his liberty.
       I'll tell you what: I think it is our way,
       If we will keep in favor with the king,
80   To be her men and wear her livery.
81   The jealous o'erworn widow and herself,
82   Since that our brother dubbed them gentlewomen,
83   Are mighty gossips in our monarchy.

BRAKENBURY

       I beseech your graces both to pardon me:
85   His majesty hath straitly given in charge
       That no man shall have private conference,
       Of what degree soever, with your brother.

RICHARD

88   Even so? An't please your worship, Brakenbury,
       You may partake of anything we say.
90   We speak no treason, man. We say the king
       Is wise and virtuous, and his noble queen
92   Well struck in years, fair, and not jealous.
       We say that Shore's wife hath a pretty foot,
       A cherry lip, a bonny eye, a passing pleasing tongue;
       And that the queen's kindred are made gentlefolks.
       How say you, sir? Can you deny all this?

---

72 *night-walking heralds* i.e., secret messengers (agents of assignation)   73
Mistress Shore Jane Shore, mistress of Edward IV   76 *her deity* i.e., Jane
Shore   77 *Lord Chamberlain* i.e., Hastings   81 *o'erworn* faded; *widow* i.e.,
Queen Elizabeth (cf. l. 109)   82 *dubbed* knighted (a malicious pairing of
Queen Elizabeth and Mistress Shore entirely without basis)   83 *gossips* busy-
bodies   85 *straitly* strictly   88 *An't* if   92 *struck* advanced

BRAKENBURY

  With this, my lord, myself have nought to do.   97

RICHARD

  Naught to do with Mistress Shore? I tell thee, fellow,   98
  He that doth naught with her (excepting one)
  Were best to do it secretly alone.   *100*

BRAKENBURY

  What one, my lord?

RICHARD

  Her husband, knave. Wouldst thou betray me?

BRAKENBURY

  I do beseech your grace to pardon me, and withal   103
  Forbear your conference with the noble duke.

CLARENCE

  We know thy charge, Brakenbury, and will obey.

RICHARD

  We are the queen's abjects, and must obey.   106
  Brother, farewell. I will unto the king;
  And whatsoe'er you will employ me in –
  Were it to call King Edward's widow sister –
  I will perform it to enfranchise you.   110
  Meantime, this deep disgrace in brotherhood   111
  Touches me deeper than you can imagine.

CLARENCE

  I know it pleaseth neither of us well.

RICHARD

  Well, your imprisonment shall not be long:
  I will deliver you, or else lie for you.   115
  Meantime, have patience.   116

CLARENCE   I must perforce. Farewell.
          Exit Clarence [with Brakenbury and Guard].

---

97 *nought* nothing **98, 99** *naught* evil (here, sexual intercourse) **103**
withal moreover **106** *abjects* most servile subjects **110** *enfranchise* release
from confinement **111–12** *disgrace ... imagine* (with an obvious double
meaning) **115** *lie for* go to prison in place of (with play on "tell lies about")
116 *perforce* of necessity

RICHARD
  Go, tread the path that thou shalt ne'er return.
  Simple plain Clarence, I do love thee so
  That I will shortly send thy soul to heaven,
120 If heaven will take the present at our hands.
  But who comes here? The new-delivered Hastings?
    Enter Lord Hastings.

HASTINGS
  Good time of day unto my gracious lord.

RICHARD
  As much unto my good Lord Chamberlain.
  Well are you welcome to this open air.
125 How hath your lordship brooked imprisonment?

HASTINGS
  With patience, noble lord, as prisoners must.
  But I shall live, my lord, to give them thanks
  That were the cause of my imprisonment.

RICHARD
  No doubt, no doubt; and so shall Clarence too,
130 For they that were your enemies are his
  And have prevailed as much on him as you.

HASTINGS
  More pity that the eagles should be mewed,
  Whiles kites and buzzards prey at liberty.

RICHARD
134 What news abroad?

HASTINGS
  No news so bad abroad as this at home:
  The king is sickly, weak, and melancholy,
137 And his physicians fear him mightily.

RICHARD
  Now, by Saint John, that news is bad indeed!
139 O, he hath kept an evil diet long
140 And overmuch consumed his royal person.
  'Tis very grievous to be thought upon.

---

125 *brooked* tolerated 134 *abroad* around 137 *fear* fear for 139 *diet* way of life

Where is he? In his bed?

HASTINGS He is.

RICHARD

Go you before, and I will follow you.   *Exit Hastings.*
He cannot live, I hope, and must not die
Till George be packed with post horse up to heaven.   146
I'll in to urge his hatred more to Clarence   147
With lies well steeled with weighty arguments;   148
And, if I fail not in my deep intent,
Clarence hath not another day to live: 150
Which done, God take King Edward to his mercy
And leave the world for me to bustle in!
For then I'll marry Warwick's youngest daughter.   153
What though I killed her husband and her father?
The readiest way to make the wench amends
Is to become her husband and her father:
The which will I – not all so much for love
As for another secret close intent   158
By marrying her which I must reach unto.
But yet I run before my horse to market: 160
Clarence still breathes; Edward still lives and reigns;
When they are gone, then must I count my gains. *Exit.*

*

∾ **I.2** *Enter [Gentlemen bearing] the corpse of Henry the*
Sixth [in an open coffin], with Halberds to guard it,
Lady Anne being the mourner [attended by Tressel
and Berkeley].

ANNE

Set down, set down your honorable load –
If honor may be shrouded in a hearse –

---

146 *with post horse* i.e., the quickest way 147 *urge . . . to* incite his anger
more against 148 *steeled* strengthened as with iron 153 *Warwick's youngest
daughter* Lady Anne Neville (betrothed, not married, to Prince Edward, son
of Henry VI; Shakespeare makes her his widow) 158 *intent* plan
    I.2 (No clear textual indication of the setting.) s.d. *Halberds* halberdiers
(guards, carrying halberds; see l. 40)

3   Whilst I awhile obsequiously lament
     Th' untimely fall of virtuous Lancaster.
          [The Bearers set down the coffin.]
5   Poor key-cold figure of a holy king,
     Pale ashes of the house of Lancaster,
     Thou bloodless remnant of that royal blood,
     Be it lawful that I invocate thy ghost
     To hear the lamentations of poor Anne,
10   Wife to thy Edward, to thy slaughtered son,
     Stabbed by the selfsame hand that made these wounds.
     Lo, in these windows that let forth thy life
13   I pour the helpless balm of my poor eyes.
     O, cursèd be the hand that made these holes.
     Cursèd the heart that had the heart to do it.
     Cursèd the blood that let this blood from hence.
17   More direful hap betide that hated wretch
     That makes us wretched by the death of thee
     Than I can wish to wolves – to spiders, toads,
20   Or any creeping venomed thing that lives.
     If ever he have child, abortive be it,
22   Prodigious, and untimely brought to light,
     Whose ugly and unnatural aspect
     May fright the hopeful mother at the view,
25   And that be heir to his unhappiness.
     If ever he have wife, let her be made
     More miserable by the death of him
     Than I am made by my young lord and thee.
29   Come, now towards Chertsey with your holy load,
30   Taken from Paul's to be interrèd there.
          [The Bearers take up the coffin.]
31   And still as you are weary of this weight,
32   Rest you, whiles I lament King Henry's corpse.

---

3 *obsequiously* in a manner fitting a funeral 5 *key-cold* very cold (as a metal
key) 13 *helpless* affording no help 17 *hap betide* fortune befall 22 *Prodigious* unnatural, monstrous 25 *unhappiness* innate evil 29 *Chertsey* the
monastery of Chertsey near London 30 *Paul's* Saint Paul's Cathedral, London 31 *still as* whenever 32 *whiles I lament* during which time I will
lament

Enter Richard Duke of Gloucester.

RICHARD
Stay, you that bear the corpse, and set it down.

ANNE
What black magician conjures up this fiend
To stop devoted charitable deeds?

RICHARD
Villains, set down the corpse, or, by Saint Paul,
I'll make a corpse of him that disobeys!

HALBERD
My lord, stand back, and let the coffin pass.

RICHARD
Unmannered dog, stand thou, when I command!   39
Advance thy halberd higher than my breast,   40
Or, by Saint Paul, I'll strike thee to my foot
And spurn upon thee, beggar, for thy boldness.   42
[The Bearers set down the coffin.]

ANNE
What, do you tremble? Are you all afraid?
Alas, I blame you not, for you are mortal,
And mortal eyes cannot endure the devil.
Avaunt, thou dreadful minister of hell!   46
Thou hadst but power over his mortal body;
His soul thou canst not have. Therefore, be gone.

RICHARD
Sweet saint, for charity, be not so curst.   49

ANNE
Foul devil, for God's sake, hence and trouble us not,   50
For thou hast made the happy earth thy hell,   51
Filled it with cursing cries and deep exclaims.
If thou delight to view thy heinous deeds,
Behold this pattern of thy butcheries.   54
O gentlemen, see, see! Dead Henry's wounds

---

39 *stand* halt   40 *Advance . . . breast* raise your halberd (a long-handled poleax with a pike attached) to upright position   42 *spurn upon* stamp under foot   46 *Avaunt* be gone   49 *curst* shrewish   51 *happy* naturally pleasant   54 *pattern* example

56 Open their congealed mouths and bleed afresh.
Blush, blush, thou lump of foul deformity,
58 For 'tis thy presence that exhales this blood
From cold and empty veins where no blood dwells.
60 Thy deeds inhuman and unnatural
Provokes this deluge most unnatural.
O God, which this blood mad'st, revenge his death.
O earth, which this blood drink'st, revenge his death.
Either heav'n with lightning strike the murd'rer dead,
65 Or earth gape open wide and eat him quick,
As thou dost swallow up this good king's blood
Which his hell-governed arm hath butcherèd!

RICHARD
Lady, you know no rules of charity,
Which renders good for bad, blessings for curses.

ANNE
70 Villain, thou know'st nor law of God nor man.
No beast so fierce but knows some touch of pity.

RICHARD
But I know none, and therefore am no beast.

ANNE
O wonderful, when devils tells the truth!

RICHARD
More wonderful, when angels are so angry.
Vouchsafe, divine perfection of a woman,
Of these supposèd crimes to give me leave
77 By circumstance but to acquit myself.

ANNE
78 Vouchsafe, diffused infection of a man,
Of these known evils, but to give me leave
80 By circumstance t' accuse thy cursèd self.

RICHARD
Fairer than tongue can name thee, let me have

---

56 *bleed afresh* (in popular belief the wounds of a murdered man bled in the presence of the murderer) 58 *exhales* draws out 65 *quick* alive 77 *circumstance* detailed argument 78 *diffused infection* shapeless plague (more for sound than sense; cf. l. 75: *Vouchsafe . . . woman*)

Some patient leisure to excuse myself.

ANNE
Fouler than heart can think thee, thou canst make
No excuse current but to hang thyself.   84

RICHARD
By such despair I should accuse myself.

ANNE
And by despairing shalt thou stand excused
For doing worthy vengeance on thyself
That didst unworthy slaughter upon others.

RICHARD
Say that I slew them not?

ANNE   Then say they were not slain.
But dead they are, and, devilish slave, by thee.   90

RICHARD
I did not kill your husband.

ANNE   Why, then he is alive.

RICHARD
Nay, he is dead, and slain by Edward's hands.

ANNE
In thy foul throat thou liest. Queen Margaret saw   93
Thy murd'rous falchion smoking in his blood,   94
The which thou once didst bend against her breast,   95
But that thy brothers beat aside the point.

RICHARD
I was provokèd by her sland'rous tongue
That laid their guilt upon my guiltless shoulders.

ANNE
Thou wast provokèd by thy bloody mind
That never dream'st on aught but butcheries.   100
Didst thou not kill this king?

RICHARD   I grant ye.

ANNE
Dost grant me, hedgehog? Then God grant me too

---

84 *current* authentic or acceptable 93–94 *In . . . blood* (in *Henry VI, Part 3*
Edward IV and Richard both stabbed the prince) 94 *falchion* slightly
hooked sword 95 *bend* turn

Thou mayst be damnèd for that wicked deed!
O, he was gentle, mild, and virtuous!
RICHARD
The better for the King of Heaven that hath him.
ANNE
He is in heaven, where thou shalt never come.
RICHARD
107   Let him thank me that holp to send him thither,
For he was fitter for that place than earth.
ANNE
And thou unfit for any place, but hell.
RICHARD
110   Yes, one place else, if you will hear me name it.
ANNE
Some dungeon.
RICHARD   Your bedchamber.
ANNE
Ill rest betide the chamber where thou liest.
RICHARD
So will it, madam, till I lie with you.
ANNE
I hope so.
RICHARD   I know so. But, gentle Lady Anne,
To leave this keen encounter of our wits
And fall something into a slower method –
117   Is not the causer of the timeless deaths
Of these Plantagenets, Henry and Edward,
As blameful as the executioner?
ANNE
120   Thou wast the cause and most accursed effect.
RICHARD
Your beauty was the cause of that effect –
Your beauty, that did haunt me in my sleep
To undertake the death of all the world,
So I might live one hour in your sweet bosom.

_____

107 *holp* helped 117 *timeless* untimely 120 *effect* i.e., *executioner* (l. 119)
or efficient agent

ANNE

  If I thought that, I tell thee, homicide,   125
  These nails should rend that beauty from my cheeks.

RICHARD

  These eyes could not endure that beauty's wrack;   127
  You should not blemish it, if I stood by.
  As all the world is cheerèd by the sun,
  So I by that. It is my day, my life.   130

ANNE

  Black night o'ershade thy day, and death thy life.

RICHARD

  Curse not thyself, fair creature – thou art both.

ANNE

  I would I were, to be revenged on thee.

RICHARD

  It is a quarrel most unnatural,
  To be revenged on him that loveth thee.

ANNE

  It is a quarrel just and reasonable,
  To be revenged on him that killed my husband.

RICHARD

  He that bereft thee, lady, of thy husband,
  Did it to help thee to a better husband.

ANNE

  His better doth not breathe upon the earth.   140

RICHARD

  He lives, that loves thee better than he could.

ANNE

  Name him.

RICHARD   Plantagenet.

ANNE   Why, that was he.

RICHARD

  The selfsame name, but one of better nature.

ANNE

  Where is he?

RICHARD   Here.

---

125 *homicide* murderer 127 *wrack* ruin

[She] spits at him. Why dost thou spit at me?

ANNE

Would it were mortal poison for thy sake.

RICHARD

Never came poison from so sweet a place.

ANNE

147   Never hung poison on a fouler toad.
Out of my sight! Thou dost infect mine eyes.

RICHARD

149   Thine eyes, sweet lady, have infected mine.

ANNE

150   Would they were basilisks to strike thee dead.

RICHARD

151   I would they were, that I might die at once,
For now they kill me with a living death.
Those eyes of thine from mine have drawn salt tears,
154   Shamed their aspects with store of childish drops:
These eyes, which never shed remorseful tear –
156   No, when my father York and Edward wept
157   To hear the piteous moan that Rutland made
158   When black-faced Clifford shook his sword at him;
159   Nor when thy warlike father, like a child,
160   Told the sad story of my father's death
And twenty times made pause to sob and weep,
That all the standers-by had wet their cheeks
Like trees bedashed with rain – in that sad time
My manly eyes did scorn an humble tear,
And what these sorrows could not thence exhale,
Thy beauty hath, and made them blind with weeping.
I never sued to friend nor enemy;
168   My tongue could never learn sweet smoothing word

---

147 *poison . . . toad* (toads were considered venomous)   149 *eyes . . . mine*
(the eyes were believed to be the entry ports of love)   150 *basilisks* fabulous
reptiles capable of killing with a look   151 *at once* once and for all   154 *aspects* glances   156 *Edward* Richard's brother, Edward IV   157–58
To . . . him (see *Henry VI, Part 3*, I.3)   158 *black-faced* gloomy, evilly portentous   159 *thy . . . father* Richard Neville, Earl of Warwick, known as the
"king maker"   168 *smoothing* flattering

But, now thy beauty is proposed my fee,
My proud heart sues, and prompts my tongue to speak.   *170*
   She looks scornfully at him.
Teach not thy lip such scorn, for it was made
For kissing, lady, not for such contempt.
If thy revengeful heart cannot forgive,
Lo, here I lend thee this sharp-pointed sword,
Which if thou please to hide in this true breast
And let the soul forth that adoreth thee,
I lay it naked to the deadly stroke   *177*
And humbly beg the death upon my knee.   *178*
   He [kneels and] lays his breast open. She offers at [it]
   with his sword.
Nay, do not pause, for I did kill King Henry —
But 'twas thy beauty that provokèd me.   *180*
Nay, now dispatch: 'twas I that stabbed young Edward —
But 'twas thy heavenly face that set me on.   *182*
   She falls the sword.
Take up the sword again, or take up me.

ANNE
Arise, dissembler. *[He rises.]* Though I wish thy death,
I will not be thy executioner.

RICHARD
Then bid me kill myself, and I will do it.

ANNE
I have already.

RICHARD   That was in thy rage.
Speak it again, and even with the word
This hand, which for thy love did kill thy love,
Shall for thy love kill a far truer love;   *190*
To both their deaths shalt thou be accessary.

ANNE
I would I knew thy heart.

RICHARD
'Tis figured in my tongue.

---

177 *naked* (1) bare, (2) unarmed **178 s.d.** *open* bare; *offers* prepares to
thrust **182 s.d.** *falls* drops

ANNE
I fear me both are false.

RICHARD
Then never man was true.

ANNE
Well, well, put up your sword.

RICHARD
Say then my peace is made.

ANNE
That shalt thou know hereafter.

RICHARD
But shall I live in hope?

ANNE
200   All men, I hope, live so.

RICHARD
201   Vouchsafe to wear this ring.

ANNE
To take is not to give.
    [Richard slips the ring on her finger.]

RICHARD
Look how my ring encompasseth thy finger,
Even so thy breast encloseth my poor heart.
Wear both of them, for both of them are thine.
206   And if thy poor devoted servant may
But beg one favor at thy gracious hand,
Thou dost confirm his happiness for ever.

ANNE   What is it?

RICHARD
210   That it may please you leave these sad designs
To him that hath most cause to be a mourner,
212   And presently repair to Crosby House,
Where – after I have solemnly interred
At Chertsey monast'ry this noble king
And wet his grave with my repentant tears –

---

201 *Vouchsafe* consent   206 *servant* lover   212 *presently* at once; *Crosby House* (one of Richard's London houses)

I will with all expedient duty see you.   216
For divers unknown reasons I beseech you,   217
Grant me this boon.

ANNE
With all my heart, and much it joys me too
To see you are become so penitent.   220
Tressel and Berkeley, go along with me.

RICHARD
Bid me farewell.   222

ANNE   'Tis more than you deserve;
But since you teach me how to flatter you,
Imagine I have said farewell already.
        Exeunt two [Tressel and Berkeley], with Anne.

RICHARD
Sirs, take up the corpse.

GENTLEMAN   Towards Chertsey, noble lord?

RICHARD
No, to Whitefriars – there attend my coming.   226
                Exit [Guard with Bearers and] corpse.
Was ever woman in this humor wooed?
Was ever woman in this humor won?
I'll have her, but I will not keep her long.
What, I that killed her husband and his father,   230
To take her in her heart's extremest hate,
With curses in her mouth, tears in her eyes,
The bleeding witness of my hatred by,
Having God, her conscience, and these bars against
    me,
And I no friends to back my suit withal
But the plain devil and dissembling looks?
And yet to win her, all the world to nothing!   237
Ha!
Hath she forgot already that brave prince,

---

216 *expedient* speedy 217 *unknown* secret 222 *'Tis . . . deserve* i.e., to fare
well is more than you deserve 226 *Whitefriars* a Carmelite priory, south of
Fleet Street, London 237 *all . . . nothing* all odds against me

240 Edward, her lord, whom I, some three months since,
241 Stabbed in my angry mood at Tewkesbury?
A sweeter and a lovelier gentleman,
243 Framed in the prodigality of nature,
Young, valiant, wise, and no doubt right royal,
The spacious world cannot again afford;
246 And will she yet abase her eyes on me,
247 That cropped the golden prime of this sweet prince
And made her widow to a woeful bed?
249 On me, whose all not equals Edward's moiety?
250 On me, that halts and am misshapen thus?
251 My dukedom to a beggarly denier,
I do mistake my person all this while!
Upon my life, she finds (although I cannot)
254 Myself to be a marvelous proper man.
255 I'll be at charges for a looking glass
And entertain a score or two of tailors
To study fashions to adorn my body.
Since I am crept in favor with myself,
I will maintain it with some little cost.
260 But first I'll turn yon fellow in his grave,
And then return lamenting to my love.
Shine out, fair sun, till I have bought a glass,
That I may see my shadow as I pass. *Exit.*

*

∾ **I.3** *Enter the Queen Mother [Elizabeth], Lord Rivers,
[Marquess of Dorset,] and Lord Grey.*

RIVERS
Have patience, madam, there's no doubt his majesty

---

241 *Tewkesbury* (scene of the battle in which the Lancastrians were finally
defeated and Prince Edward killed) 243 *prodigality* profuseness 246 *abase*
cast down or make base 247 *cropped . . . prince* i.e., cut him off in the
flower of youth 249 *moiety* half 251 *denier* copper coin, twelfth of a sou
(dissyllabic) 254 *marvelous proper* wonderfully handsome 255 *at charges
for* at the expense of 260 *in* into
I.3 The royal palace

Will soon recover his accustomed health.

GREY
In that you brook it ill, it makes him worse.   3
Therefore for God's sake entertain good comfort
And cheer his grace with quick and merry eyes.   5

QUEEN ELIZABETH
If he were dead, what would betide on me?   6

GREY
No other harm but loss of such a lord.

QUEEN ELIZABETH
The loss of such a lord includes all harms.

GREY
The heavens have blessed you with a goodly son
To be your comforter when he is gone.   10

QUEEN ELIZABETH
Ah, he is young, and his minority
Is put unto the trust of Richard Gloucester,
A man that loves not me, nor none of you.

RIVERS
Is it concluded he shall be Protector?

QUEEN ELIZABETH
It is determined, not concluded yet;   15
But so it must be, if the king miscarry.
        Enter Buckingham and [Stanley Earl of] Derby.

GREY
Here come the lords of Buckingham and Derby.

BUCKINGHAM
Good time of day unto your royal grace!

DERBY
God make your majesty joyful, as you have been!

QUEEN ELIZABETH
The Countess Richmond, good my Lord of Derby,   20
To your good prayer will scarcely say "Amen."

---

3 *brook* endure 5 *quick* lively 6 *betide on* happen to 15 *determined, not
concluded* resolved, not officially decreed 20 *Countess Richmond* Margaret
Beaufort, mother of Henry Tudor, the Earl of Richmond (later Henry VII),
now wife of Lord Stanley, Earl of Derby (as a Lancastrian, she would not
wish well to Yorkists)

Yet, Derby, notwithstanding she's your wife
And loves not me, be you, good lord, assured
I hate not you for her proud arrogance.

DERBY
I do beseech you, either not believe
The envious slanders of her false accusers,
Or, if she be accused on true report,
Bear with her weakness, which I think proceeds
29 From wayward sickness, and no grounded malice.

QUEEN ELIZABETH
30 Saw you the king today, my Lord of Derby?

DERBY
31 But now the Duke of Buckingham and I
Are come from visiting his majesty.

QUEEN ELIZABETH
What likelihood of his amendment, lords?

BUCKINGHAM
Madam, good hope; his grace speaks cheerfully.

QUEEN ELIZABETH
God grant him health! Did you confer with him?

BUCKINGHAM
36 Ay, madam: he desires to make atonement
Between the Duke of Gloucester and your brothers,
And between them and my Lord Chamberlain,
And sent to warn them to his royal presence.

QUEEN ELIZABETH
40 Would all were well! But that will never be.
41 I fear our happiness is at the height.
        Enter Richard [and Lord Hastings].

RICHARD
They do me wrong, and I will not endure it.
Who is it that complains unto the king
That I forsooth am stern and love them not?
By holy Paul, they love his grace but lightly

---

29 *wayward sickness* illness not yielding readily to treatment **31** *But now*
just now **36** *atonement* reconciliation **41** *happiness . . . height* good fortune has reached its peak

That fill his ears with such dissentious rumors.
Because I cannot flatter and look fair,
Smile in men's faces, smooth, deceive, and cog,   48
Duck with French nods and apish courtesy,   49
I must be held a rancorous enemy.   50
Cannot a plain man live and think no harm,
But thus his simple truth must be abused
With silken, sly, insinuating jacks?   53

GREY
To who in all this presence speaks your grace?

RICHARD
To thee, that hast nor honesty nor grace.   55
When have I injured thee? when done thee wrong?
Or thee? or thee? or any of your faction?
A plague upon you all! His royal grace
(Whom God preserve better than you would wish!)
Cannot be quiet scarce a breathing while   60
But you must trouble him with lewd complaints.   61

QUEEN ELIZABETH
Brother of Gloucester, you mistake the matter:
The king, on his own royal disposition,   63
And not provoked by any suitor else,
Aiming belike at your interior hatred,
That in your outward action shows itself
Against my children, brothers, and myself,
Makes him to send, that he may learn the ground
Of your ill will, and thereby to remove it.

RICHARD
I cannot tell. The world is grown so bad   70
That wrens make prey where eagles dare not perch.
Since every jack became a gentleman,
There's many a gentle person made a jack.

---

48 *smooth* flatter; *cog* cheat   49 *French nods* elaborate bows; *apish* imitative   53 *jacks* low-bred, worthless fellows (with play on French "Jacques")   55 *grace* sense of duty or virtue (with play on the title *your grace*, l. 54)   60 *breathing while* i.e., long enough to catch his breath   61 *lewd* wicked   63–68 *The king . . . send* (syntax confused; for *Makes him to send* understand "sends")   63 *disposition* inclination

QUEEN ELIZABETH
Come, come, we know your meaning, brother Glouces-
ter:
You envy my advancement and my friends'.
God grant we never may have need of you!
RICHARD
Meantime, God grants that I have need of you.
Our brother is imprisoned by your means,
Myself disgraced, and the nobility
80 Held in contempt, while great promotions
Are daily given to ennoble those
82 That scarce, some two days since, were worth a noble.
QUEEN ELIZABETH
83 By him that raised me to this careful height
84 From that contented hap which I enjoyed,
I never did incense his majesty
Against the Duke of Clarence, but have been
An earnest advocate to plead for him.
My lord, you do me shameful injury
89 Falsely to draw me in these vile suspects.
RICHARD
90 You may deny that you were not the mean
Of my Lord Hastings' late imprisonment.
RIVERS
She may, my lord, for –
RICHARD
She may, Lord Rivers! why, who knows not so?
She may do more, sir, than denying that:
She may help you to many fair preferments,
And then deny her aiding hand therein
And lay those honors on your high desert.
98 What may she not? She may – ay, marry, may she –
RIVERS
What, marry, may she?

---

82 *noble* (1) gold coin, worth one third of a pound, (2) nobleman 83 *careful* full of anxiety 84 *hap* fortune 89 *in* into; *suspects* suspicions 98
marry indeed (with play on "wed")

RICHARD
  What, marry, may she? Marry with a king,   100
  A bachelor and a handsome stripling too:
  Iwis your grandam had a worser match.   102

QUEEN ELIZABETH
  My Lord of Gloucester, I have too long borne
  Your blunt upbraidings and your bitter scoffs.
  By heaven, I will acquaint his majesty
  Of those gross taunts that oft I have endured.
  I had rather be a country servant maid
  Than a great queen with this condition,
  To be so baited, scorned, and stormèd at: 109
      Enter old Queen Margaret [behind].
  Small joy have I in being England's queen.   110

QUEEN MARGARET *[Aside]*
  And lessened be that small, God I beseech him!
  Thy honor, state, and seat is due to me.   112

RICHARD
  What? Threat you me with telling of the king?
  Tell him, and spare not. Look, what I have said
  I will avouch't in presence of the king.
  I dare adventure to be sent to th' Tower.
  'Tis time to speak; my pains are quite forgot.   117

QUEEN MARGARET *[Aside]*
  Out, devil! I do remember them too well:
  Thou kill'dst my husband Henry in the Tower,
  And Edward, my poor son, at Tewkesbury.   120

RICHARD
  Ere you were queen, ay, or your husband king,
  I was a packhorse in his great affairs,   122
  A weeder-out of his proud adversaries,
  A liberal rewarder of his friends.
  To royalize his blood I spent mine own.

---

102 *Iwis* certainly   **109** *baited* taunted; *s.d. Queen Margaret* widow of
Henry VI, symbol of the defeat of the Lancastrians   **112** *state* high rank (as
queen); *seat* throne   **117** *pains* efforts on his behalf   **122** *packhorse* beast of
burden, drudge

QUEEN MARGARET *[Aside]*
Ay, and much better blood than his or thine.

RICHARD

127 In all which time you and your husband Grey
128 Were factious for the house of Lancaster;
And, Rivers, so were you. Was not your husband
130 In Margaret's battle at Saint Albans slain?
Let me put in your minds, if you forget,
What you have been ere this, and what you are;
Withal, what I have been, and what I am.

QUEEN MARGARET *[Aside]*
A murd'rous villain, and so still thou art.

RICHARD

135 Poor Clarence did forsake his father Warwick –
136 Ay, and forswore himself – which Jesu pardon! –

QUEEN MARGARET *[Aside]*
Which God revenge!

RICHARD

To fight on Edward's party for the crown,
139 And for his meed, poor lord, he is mewed up.
140 I would to God my heart were flint like Edward's,
Or Edward's soft and pitiful like mine:
I am too childish-foolish for this world.

QUEEN MARGARET *[Aside]*
Hie thee to hell for shame, and leave this world,
144 Thou cacodemon, there thy kingdom is.

RIVERS

My Lord of Gloucester, in those busy days
Which here you urge to prove us enemies,
We followed then our lord, our sovereign king.
So should we you, if you should be our king.

127–30 *husband . . . Saint Albans* (the queen's first husband, Sir John Grey, was killed at the battle of Saint Albans fighting against the Yorkists) 128 *factious* partisan 135 *father Warwick* (Clarence married Warwick's daughter, Isabella Neville, sister of Lady Anne in *Richard III,* and temporarily went over to the Lancastrian side) 136 *forswore* (by returning to the Yorkist side) 139 *meed* reward; *mewed up* imprisoned 144 *cacodemon* evil spirit

RICHARD
  If I should be? I had rather be a peddler.
  Far be it from my heart, the thought thereof.   *150*
QUEEN ELIZABETH
  As little joy, my lord, as you suppose
  You should enjoy, were you this country's king –
  As little joy you may suppose in me
  That I enjoy, being the queen thereof.
QUEEN MARGARET *[Aside]*
  Ah, little joy enjoys the queen thereof,
  For I am she, and altogether joyless.
  I can no longer hold me patient.
      [Comes forward.]
  Hear me, you wrangling pirates, that fall out
  In sharing that which you have pilled from me.   *159*
  Which of you trembles not that looks on me?   *160*
  If not that I am queen, you bow like subjects,   *161*
  Yet that by you deposed, you quake like rebels.
  Ah, gentle villain, do not turn away.
RICHARD
  Foul wrinkled witch, what mak'st thou in my sight?   *164*
QUEEN MARGARET
  But repetition of what thou hast marred:
  That will I make before I let thee go.
RICHARD
  Wert thou not banishèd on pain of death?
QUEEN MARGARET
  I was, but I do find more pain in banishment
  Than death can yield me here by my abode.
  A husband and a son thou ow'st to me –   *170*
      [To Queen Elizabeth]
  And thou a kingdom – all of you allegiance.
  This sorrow that I have, by right is yours,

---

159 *pilled* plundered 161–62 *that . . . that* because . . . because 164 *mak'st thou* are you doing (but Margaret replies as if Richard had meant "What are you making?")

And all the pleasures you usurp are mine.

RICHARD

174   The curse my noble father laid on thee
When thou didst crown his warlike brows with paper
And with thy scorns drew'st rivers from his eyes
177   And then, to dry them, gav'st the duke a clout
Steeped in the faultless blood of pretty Rutland –
His curses then, from bitterness of soul
180   Denounced against thee, are all fall'n upon thee,
And God, not we, hath plagued thy bloody deed.

QUEEN ELIZABETH

So just is God, to right the innocent.

HASTINGS

O, 'twas the foulest deed to slay that babe,
And the most merciless, that e'er was heard of.

RIVERS

Tyrants themselves wept when it was reported.

DORSET

No man but prophesied revenge for it.

BUCKINGHAM

Northumberland, then present, wept to see it.

QUEEN MARGARET

What? were you snarling all before I came,
Ready to catch each other by the throat,
190   And turn you all your hatred now on me?
Did York's dread curse prevail so much with heaven
That Henry's death, my lovely Edward's death,
Their kingdom's loss, my woeful banishment,
194   Should all but answer for that peevish brat?
Can curses pierce the clouds and enter heaven?
196   Why then, give way, dull clouds, to my quick curses.
Though not by war, by surfeit die your king,
As ours by murder, to make him a king.
    [To Queen Elizabeth]
Edward thy son, that now is Prince of Wales,

174–81 *The curse . . . deed* (see *Henry VI, Part 3*, I.4) 177 *clout* handkerchief 194 *but answer for* merely be equal to 196 *quick* full of life

For Edward our son, that was Prince of Wales,   200
Die in his youth by like untimely violence.
Thyself a queen, for me that was a queen,
Outlive thy glory, like my wretched self.
Long mayst thou live to wail thy children's death
And see another, as I see thee now,
Decked in thy rights as thou art stalled in mine.   206
Long die thy happy days before thy death,
And, after many lengthened hours of grief,
Die neither mother, wife, nor England's queen.
Rivers and Dorset, you were standers-by,   210
And so wast thou, Lord Hastings, when my son
Was stabbed with bloody daggers. God, I pray him
That none of you may live his natural age,
But by some unlooked accident cut off.

RICHARD
Have done thy charm, thou hateful withered hag.   215

QUEEN MARGARET
And leave out thee? Stay, dog, for thou shalt hear me.
If heaven have any grievous plague in store
Exceeding those that I can wish upon thee,
O, let them keep it till thy sins be ripe,
And then hurl down their indignation   220
On thee, the troubler of the poor world's peace.
The worm of conscience still begnaw thy soul.
Thy friends suspect for traitors while thou liv'st,
And take deep traitors for thy dearest friends.
No sleep close up that deadly eye of thine,   225
Unless it be while some tormenting dream
Affrights thee with a hell of ugly devils.
Thou elvish-marked, abortive, rooting hog,   228
Thou that wast sealed in thy nativity

---

206 *stalled* installed 210–12 *Rivers . . . daggers* (none of them was present
in the scene as shown in *Henry VI, Part 3*, though they were according to
Shakespeare's sources) 215 *charm* magic spell (Richard addresses Margaret
as a witch; cf. l. 164) 225 *deadly* killing (like the eye of a basilisk; cf. I.2.
150) 228 *elvish-marked* marked at birth by evil fairies; *hog* (Richard's badge
was a boar)

230 The slave of nature and the son of hell,
231 Thou slander of thy heavy mother's womb,
     Thou loathèd issue of thy father's loins,
     Thou rag of honor, thou detested –

RICHARD
     Margaret.

QUEEN MARGARET   Richard!

RICHARD   Ha?

QUEEN MARGARET   I call thee not.

RICHARD
235 I cry thee mercy then, for I did think
     That thou hadst called me all these bitter names.

QUEEN MARGARET
     Why, so I did, but looked for no reply.
238 O, let me make the period to my curse.

RICHARD
     'Tis done by me, and ends in "Margaret."

QUEEN ELIZABETH
240 Thus have you breathed your curse against yourself.

QUEEN MARGARET
241 Poor painted queen, vain flourish of my fortune.
242 Why strew'st thou sugar on that bottled spider
     Whose deadly web ensnareth thee about?
     Fool, fool! thou whet'st a knife to kill thyself.
     The day will come that thou shalt wish for me
     To help thee curse this poisonous bunch-backed toad.

HASTINGS
247 False-boding woman, end thy frantic curse,
248 Lest to thy harm thou move our patience.

QUEEN MARGARET
     Foul shame upon you, you have all moved mine.

RIVERS
250 Were you well served, you would be taught your duty.

---

230 *slave of nature* (because deformed from birth) 231 *heavy* sad 235 *cry thee mercy* beg your pardon (sarcasm) 238 *period* end (as of a sentence; cf. II.1.44) 241 *painted queen* queen in outward show; *flourish* meaningless decoration 242 *bottled* swollen (hunchbacked, full of venom) 247 *False-boding* prophesying falsely 248 *patience* (trisyllabic)

QUEEN MARGARET
  To serve me well, you all should do me duty,
  Teach me to be your queen, and you my subjects.
  O, serve me well, and teach yourselves that duty.
DORSET
  Dispute not with her; she is lunatic.
QUEEN MARGARET
  Peace, Master Marquess, you are malapert.   255
  Your fire-new stamp of honor is scarce current.   256
  O, that your young nobility could judge   257
  What 'twere to lose it and be miserable.
  They that stand high have many blasts to shake them,
  And if they fall, they dash themselves to pieces.   260
RICHARD
  Good counsel, marry! Learn it, learn it, Marquess.
DORSET
  It touches you, my lord, as much as me.
RICHARD
  Ay, and much more; but I was born so high.
  Our aerie buildeth in the cedar's top   264
  And dallies with the wind and scorns the sun.   265
QUEEN MARGARET
  And turns the sun to shade – alas! alas!
  Witness my son, now in the shade of death,
  Whose bright outshining beams thy cloudy wrath
  Hath in eternal darkness folded up.
  Your aerie buildeth in our aerie's nest.   270
  O God, that seest it, do not suffer it;
  As it is won with blood, lost be it so.
BUCKINGHAM
  Peace, peace, for shame, if not for charity.
QUEEN MARGARET
  Urge neither charity nor shame to me:

---

255 *malapert* impudent 256 *Your . . . current* your title is so new-coined
that it is scarcely legal tender 257 *young nobility* new state of honor 264
aerie brood of young eagles (the sons of York) 265–66 *sun . . . sun* (double
play on *sun,* as king symbol and as son)

[Turning to the others]
Uncharitably with me have you dealt,
And shamefully my hopes by you are butchered.
My charity is outrage, life my shame,
And in that shame still live my sorrow's rage.

BUCKINGHAM
Have done, have done.

QUEEN MARGARET
280 O princely Buckingham, I'll kiss thy hand
In sign of league and amity with thee:
Now fair befall thee and thy noble house!
Thy garments are not spotted with our blood,
Nor thou within the compass of my curse.

BUCKINGHAM
Nor no one here, for curses never pass
The lips of those that breathe them in the air.

QUEEN MARGARET
287 I will not think but they ascend the sky
And there awake God's gentle-sleeping peace.
O Buckingham, take heed of yonder dog.
290 Look when he fawns he bites; and when he bites,
291 His venom tooth will rankle to the death.
Have not to do with him, beware of him.
Sin, death, and hell have set their marks on him,
And all their ministers attend on him.

RICHARD
What doth she say, my Lord of Buckingham?

BUCKINGHAM
Nothing that I respect, my gracious lord.

QUEEN MARGARET
What, dost thou scorn me for my gentle counsel,
And soothe the devil that I warn thee from?
O, but remember this another day,
300 When he shall split thy very heart with sorrow,
And say poor Margaret was a prophetess!

___

287 *not think but* believe 290 *Look when* whenever 291 *rankle* cause a festering wound

Live each of you the subjects to his hate,
And he to yours, and all of you to God's!   *Exit.*

BUCKINGHAM
My hair doth stand on end to hear her curses.

RIVERS
And so doth mine. I muse why she's at liberty.

RICHARD
I cannot blame her. By God's holy Mother,
She hath had too much wrong, and I repent
My part thereof that I have done to her.

QUEEN ELIZABETH
I never did her any to my knowledge.

RICHARD
Yet you have all the vantage of her wrong.   310
I was too hot to do somebody good   311
That is too cold in thinking of it now.
Marry, as for Clarence, he is well repaid;
He is franked up to fatting for his pains –   314
God pardon them that are the cause thereof.

RIVERS
A virtuous and a Christianlike conclusion,
To pray for them that have done scathe to us.   317

RICHARD
So do I ever – *(Speaks to himself.)* being well advised,
For had I cursed now, I had cursed myself.
    Enter Catesby.

CATESBY
Madam, his majesty doth call for you,   320
And for your grace, and you, my gracious lords.

QUEEN ELIZABETH
Catesby, I come. Lords, will you go with me?

RIVERS
We wait upon your grace.
                Exeunt all but [Richard of] Gloucester.

---

311 *too hot . . . good* i.e., too eager in helping Edward to the crown 314
franked . . . fatting shut in a sty for fattening (i.e., slaughter) 317 *scathe* injury

RICHARD
　　I do the wrong, and first begin to brawl.
　　The secret mischiefs that I set abroach
326　I lay unto the grievous charge of others.
　　Clarence, who I indeed have cast in darkness,
328　I do beweep to many simple gulls –
　　Namely to Derby, Hastings, Buckingham –
330　And tell them 'tis the queen and her allies
　　That stir the king against the duke my brother.
　　Now they believe it, and withal whet me
　　To be revenged on Rivers, Dorset, Grey.
　　But then I sigh, and, with a piece of Scripture,
　　Tell them that God bids us do good for evil:
　　And thus I clothe my naked villainy
337　With odd old ends stol'n forth of holy writ,
　　And seem a saint, when most I play the devil.
　　　　Enter two Murderers.
　　But soft! Here come my executioners.
340　How now, my hardy, stout, resolvèd mates!
　　Are you now going to dispatch this thing?
FIRST MURDERER
　　We are, my lord, and come to have the warrant,
　　That we may be admitted where he is.
RICHARD
　　Well thought upon; I have it here about me.
　　　　[Gives the warrant.]
　　When you have done, repair to Crosby Place.
　　But, sirs, be sudden in the execution,
　　Withal obdurate, do not hear him plead,
　　For Clarence is well-spoken, and perhaps
　　May move your hearts to pity if you mark him.
FIRST MURDERER
350　Tut, tut, my lord, we will not stand to prate.
　　Talkers are no good doers. Be assured,
　　We go to use our hands, and not our tongues.

---

326 *lay . . . of* impute as a severe accusation against 328 *gulls* fools 337 *ends* bits and pieces 350 *prate* talk idly, chatter

RICHARD
    Your eyes drop millstones when fools' eyes fall tears.   353
    I like you, lads. About your business straight.
    Go, go, dispatch.
BOTH MURDERERS We will, my noble lord.
                                              [Exeunt.]

                            *

∾ **I.4** *Enter Clarence and Keeper.*

KEEPER
    Why looks your grace so heavily today?   1
CLARENCE
    O, I have passed a miserable night,
    So full of fearful dreams, of ugly sights,
    That, as I am a Christian faithful man,   4
    I would not spend another such a night
    Though 'twere to buy a world of happy days,
    So full of dismal terror was the time.
KEEPER
    What was your dream, my lord? I pray you tell me.
CLARENCE
    Methoughts that I had broken from the Tower
    And was embarked to cross to Burgundy,   10
    And in my company my brother Gloucester,
    Who from my cabin tempted me to walk
    Upon the hatches; there we looked toward England   13
    And cited up a thousand heavy times   14
    During the wars of York and Lancaster
    That had befall'n us. As we paced along
    Upon the giddy footing of the hatches,   17
    Methought that Gloucester stumbled, and in falling
    Struck me (that thought to stay him) overboard

---

353 *fall* let fall
  I.4 The Tower of London **s.d.** *Keeper* (in Q the keeper's lines are all given
to Brakenbury, combining the two roles) 1 *heavily* sad 4 *faithful* believing in
religion 13 *hatches* movable planks forming a kind of deck 14 *cited up*
recalled 17 *giddy footing* foothold producing dizziness

20   Into the tumbling billows of the main.
      O Lord, methought what pain it was to drown,
      What dreadful noise of water in mine ears,
      What sights of ugly death within mine eyes.
      Methoughts I saw a thousand fearful wracks,
      A thousand men that fishes gnawed upon,
      Wedges of gold, great anchors, heaps of pearl,
27   Inestimable stones, unvalued jewels,
      All scattered in the bottom of the sea.
      Some lay in dead men's skulls, and in the holes
30   Where eyes did once inhabit, there were crept
      (As 'twere in scorn of eyes) reflecting gems,
      That wooed the slimy bottom of the deep
      And mocked the dead bones that lay scattered by.

KEEPER
      Had you such leisure in the time of death
      To gaze upon these secrets of the deep?

CLARENCE
      Methought I had, and often did I strive
37   To yield the ghost, but still the envious flood
      Stopped in my soul, and would not let it forth
      To find the empty, vast, and wand'ring air,
40   But smothered it within my panting bulk,
      Who almost burst to belch it in the sea.

KEEPER
      Awaked you not in this sore agony?

CLARENCE
      No, no, my dream was lengthened after life.
      O, then began the tempest to my soul.
45   I passed, methought, the melancholy flood,
46   With that sour ferryman which poets write of,
      Unto the kingdom of perpetual night.

___

27 *Inestimable . . . jewels* precious stones without number and costly ornaments (*jewels*) beyond price 37 *yield the ghost* die; *still* always 40 *bulk* body
45 *the melancholy flood* the river Styx, entrance to Hades, the underworld in
classical mythology 46 *ferryman* Charon (who ferried souls across the river
Styx)

The first that there did greet my stranger soul   48
Was my great father-in-law, renownèd Warwick,
Who spake aloud, "What scourge for perjury   50
Can this dark monarchy afford false Clarence?"
And so he vanished. Then came wand'ring by
A shadow like an angel, with bright hair   53
Dabbled in blood, and he shrieked out aloud,
"Clarence is come: false, fleeting, perjured Clarence,   55
That stabbed me in the field by Tewkesbury.
Seize on him, Furies, take him unto torment."
With that, methoughts, a legion of foul fiends
Environed me, and howlèd in mine ears   59
Such hideous cries that with the very noise   60
I trembling waked, and for a season after
Could not believe but that I was in hell,
Such terrible impression made my dream.

KEEPER
No marvel, lord, though it affrighted you;
I am afraid, methinks, to hear you tell it.

CLARENCE
Ah, keeper, keeper, I have done these things,
That now give evidence against my soul,
For Edward's sake, and see how he requites me.
O God, if my deep prayers cannot appease thee,
But thou wilt be avenged on my misdeeds,   70
Yet execute thy wrath in me alone.
O, spare my guiltless wife and my poor children.
Keeper, I prithee sit by me awhile.
My soul is heavy, and I fain would sleep.   74

KEEPER
I will, my lord. God give your grace good rest.
    [Clarence sleeps.]
    Enter Brakenbury, the Lieutenant.

---

48 *stranger* newly arrived 53 *A shadow* i.e., Edward, Prince of Wales, son of Henry VI 55 *fleeting* fickle 59 *Environed* surrounded 74 *fain would* desire to

BRAKENBURY

76 Sorrow breaks seasons and reposing hours,
    Makes the night morning and the noontide night.
    Princes have but their titles for their glories,
    An outward honor for an inward toil,
80 And for unfelt imaginations
    They often feel a world of restless cares;
    So that between their titles and low name
    There's nothing differs but the outward fame.
        Enter two Murderers.

FIRST MURDERER Ho! who's here?

BRAKENBURY
    What wouldst thou, fellow? And how cam'st thou
    hither?

FIRST MURDERER I would speak with Clarence, and I
    came hither on my legs.

BRAKENBURY What, so brief?

SECOND MURDERER 'Tis better, sir, than to be tedious.
90 Let him see our commission, and talk no more.
        [Brakenbury] reads [it].

BRAKENBURY
    I am, in this, commanded to deliver
    The noble Duke of Clarence to your hands.
    I will not reason what is meant hereby,
94 Because I will be guiltless from the meaning.
    There lies the duke asleep, and there the keys.
    I'll to the king and signify to him
    That thus I have resigned to you my charge.

FIRST MURDERER You may, sir; 'tis a point of wisdom.
    Fare you well.   *Exit [Brakenbury with Keeper].*

100 SECOND MURDERER What? Shall I stab him as he sleeps?

FIRST MURDERER No. He'll say 'twas done cowardly
    when he wakes.

---

76 *breaks seasons* disrupts normal rhythms; *reposing hours* hours proper to
sleep 80 *for unfelt imaginations* for the sake of imaginary and unreal gratifi-
cations (Dr. Johnson) 90 *commission* warrant 94 *will be* wish to be

SECOND MURDERER Why, he shall never wake until the great Judgment Day.

FIRST MURDERER Why, then he'll say we stabbed him sleeping.

SECOND MURDERER The urging of that word "judgment" hath bred a kind of remorse in me.

FIRST MURDERER What? Art thou afraid?

SECOND MURDERER Not to kill him, having a warrant, 110 but to be damned for killing him, from the which no warrant can defend me.

FIRST MURDERER I thought thou hadst been resolute.

SECOND MURDERER So I am – to let him live.

FIRST MURDERER I'll back to the Duke of Gloucester and tell him so.

SECOND MURDERER Nay, I prithee stay a little. I hope this passionate humor of mine will change. It was wont 118 to hold me but while one tells twenty. 119

FIRST MURDERER How dost thou feel thyself now? 120

SECOND MURDERER Faith, some certain dregs of conscience are yet within me.

FIRST MURDERER Remember our reward when the deed's done.

SECOND MURDERER Zounds, he dies! I had forgot the 125 reward.

FIRST MURDERER Where's thy conscience now?

SECOND MURDERER O, in the Duke of Gloucester's purse.

FIRST MURDERER When he opens his purse to give us 130 our reward, thy conscience flies out.

SECOND MURDERER 'Tis no matter; let it go. There's few or none will entertain it.

FIRST MURDERER What if it come to thee again?

SECOND MURDERER I'll not meddle with it. It makes a man a coward. A man cannot steal, but it accuseth him; a man cannot swear, but it checks him; a man cannot

---

118 *passionate* compassionate 119 *tells* counts to 125 *Zounds* by God's wounds

lie with his neighbor's wife, but it detects him. 'Tis a
blushing shame-faced spirit that mutinies in a man's
140   bosom. It fills a man full of obstacles. It made me once
restore a purse of gold that by chance I found. It beggars any man that keeps it. It is turned out of towns
and cities for a dangerous thing, and every man that
means to live well endeavors to trust to himself and live
without it.

FIRST MURDERER   Zounds, 'tis even now at my elbow,
persuading me not to kill the duke.

SECOND MURDERER   Take the devil in thy mind, and be-
149   lieve him not. He would insinuate with thee but to
150   make thee sigh.

FIRST MURDERER   I am strong-framed; he cannot prevail
with me.

153   SECOND MURDERER   Spoke like a tall man that respects
thy reputation. Come, shall we fall to work?

155   FIRST MURDERER   Take him on the costard with the hilts
156   of thy sword, and then throw him into the malmsey
butt in the next room.

158   SECOND MURDERER   O excellent device! and make a sop
of him.

160   FIRST MURDERER   Soft! he wakes.

SECOND MURDERER   Strike!

FIRST MURDERER   No, we'll reason with him.

CLARENCE
Where art thou, keeper? Give me a cup of wine.

SECOND MURDERER
You shall have wine enough, my lord, anon.

CLARENCE
In God's name, what art thou?

FIRST MURDERER
A man, as you are.

---

149 *him* i.e., your *conscience; insinuate* ingratiate himself   150 *make thee
sigh* cause you grief   153 *tall* valiant   155 *costard* head   156–57 *malmsey
butt* barrel of malmsey wine (a strong sweet wine)   158 *sop* wafer floated in
a cup of wine

CLARENCE
But not as I am, royal.

FIRST MURDERER
Nor you as we are, loyal.

CLARENCE
Thy voice is thunder, but thy looks are humble.

FIRST MURDERER
My voice is now the king's, my looks mine own. *170*

CLARENCE
How darkly and how deadly dost thou speak. 171
Your eyes do menace me. Why look you pale?
Who sent you hither? Wherefore do you come?

BOTH
To, to, to –

CLARENCE   To murder me?

BOTH   Ay, ay.

CLARENCE
You scarcely have the hearts to tell me so,
And therefore cannot have the hearts to do it.
Wherein, my friends, have I offended you?

FIRST MURDERER
Offended us you have not, but the king.

CLARENCE
I shall be reconciled to him again.

SECOND MURDERER
Never, my lord; therefore prepare to die. *180*

CLARENCE
Are you drawn forth among a world of men 181
To slay the innocent? What is my offense?
Where is the evidence that doth accuse me?
What lawful quest have given their verdict up 184
Unto the frowning judge? or who pronounced
The bitter sentence of poor Clarence' death?
Before I be convict by course of law,
To threaten me with death is most unlawful.

---

171 *deadly* threatening death 181 *drawn . . . men* specially chosen among
all mankind 184 *quest* jury

I charge you, as you hope to have redemption
190 By Christ's dear blood shed for our grievous sins,
That you depart, and lay no hands on me.
192 The deed you undertake is damnable.

FIRST MURDERER
What we will do, we do upon command.

SECOND MURDERER
And he that hath commanded is our king.

CLARENCE
195 Erroneous vassals! The great King of Kings
Hath in the table of his law commanded
That thou shalt do no murder. Will you then
Spurn at his edict, and fulfill a man's?
Take heed, for he holds vengeance in his hand
200 To hurl upon their heads that break his law.

SECOND MURDERER
And that same vengeance doth he hurl on thee
For false forswearing and for murder too:
Thou didst receive the sacrament to fight
In quarrel of the house of Lancaster.

FIRST MURDERER
And like a traitor to the name of God
Didst break that vow, and with thy treacherous blade
Unripped'st the bowels of thy sov'reign's son.

SECOND MURDERER
Whom thou wast sworn to cherish and defend.

FIRST MURDERER
How canst thou urge God's dreadful law to us
210 When thou hast broke it in such dear degree?

CLARENCE
Alas! for whose sake did I that ill deed?
For Edward, for my brother, for his sake.
He sends you not to murder me for this,
For in that sin he is as deep as I.

---

192 *damnable* leading to damnation (for you)   195 *Erroneous vassals* mis-
guided subjects   210 *dear degree* serious measure

If God will be avengèd for the deed,
O, know you yet, he doth it publicly.
Take not the quarrel from his pow'rful arm.
He needs no indirect or lawless course
To cut off those that have offended him.

FIRST MURDERER
Who made thee then a bloody minister   220
When gallant-springing brave Plantagenet,   221
That princely novice, was struck dead by thee?   222

CLARENCE
My brother's love, the devil, and my rage.

FIRST MURDERER
Thy brother's love, our duty, and thy faults
Provoke us hither now to slaughter thee.

CLARENCE
O, if you love my brother, hate not me.
I am his brother, and I love him well.
If you are hired for meed, go back again,   228
And I will send you to my brother Gloucester,
Who shall reward you better for my life   230
Than Edward will for tidings of my death.

SECOND MURDERER
You are deceived. Your brother Gloucester hates you.

CLARENCE
O, no, he loves me and he holds me dear.
Go you to him from me.

FIRST MURDERER   Ay, so we will.

CLARENCE
Tell him, when that our princely father York
Blessed his three sons with his victorious arm
And charged us from his soul to love each other,
He little thought of this divided friendship.
Bid Gloucester think on this, and he will weep.

---

221 *gallant-springing* gallant and sprightly 222 *novice* (1) one just beginning his duties, (2) youth 228 *meed* reward

FIRST MURDERER

240 Ay, millstones, as he lessoned us to weep.

CLARENCE

241 O, do not slander him, for he is kind.

FIRST MURDERER

242 Right as snow in harvest. Come, you deceive yourself;
'Tis he that sends us to destroy you here.

CLARENCE

It cannot be, for he bewept my fortune,
And hugged me in his arms, and swore with sobs
That he would labor my delivery.

FIRST MURDERER

Why, so he doth, when he delivers you
From this earth's thralldom to the joys of heaven.

SECOND MURDERER

Make peace with God, for you must die, my lord.

CLARENCE

250 Have you that holy feeling in your souls
To counsel me to make my peace with God,
And are you yet to your own souls so blind
That you will war with God by murd'ring me?
O, sirs, consider, they that set you on
To do this deed will hate you for the deed.

SECOND MURDERER

What shall we do?

CLARENCE   Relent, and save your souls.
Which of you, if you were a prince's son,

258 Being pent from liberty, as I am now,
If two such murderers as yourselves came to you,

260 Would not entreat for life?

FIRST MURDERER

Relent? No, 'tis cowardly and womanish.

CLARENCE

Not to relent is beastly, savage, devilish.

---

241 *kind* (1) with feelings natural to a brother, (2) good 242 *Right as* just as much as 258 *pent* imprisoned

My friend, *[To Second Murderer]* I spy some pity in thy
  looks.
O, if thine eye be not a flatterer,
Come thou on my side, and entreat for me
As you would beg, were you in my distress.
A begging prince what beggar pities not?

SECOND MURDERER
Look behind you, my lord!

FIRST MURDERER
Take that! and that! *(Stabs him.)* If all this will not do,
I'll drown you in the malmsey butt within.   270
                                        Exit [with the body].

SECOND MURDERER
A bloody deed, and desperately dispatched.
How fain, like Pilate, would I wash my hands
Of this most grievous murder.
     Enter First Murderer.

FIRST MURDERER
How now? What mean'st thou that thou help'st me
  not?
By heavens, the duke shall know how slack you have
  been.

SECOND MURDERER
I would he knew that I had saved his brother!
Take thou the fee and tell him what I say,
For I repent me that the duke is slain.   *Exit.*

FIRST MURDERER
So do not I. Go, coward as thou art.
Well, I'll go hide the body in some hole   280
Till that the duke give order for his burial;
And when I have my meed, I will away,
For this will out, and then I must not stay.   *Exit.* 283

                        *

---

283 *this will out* i.e., murder will out (proverbial)

∽ **II.1** *Flourish. Enter the King [Edward], sick, the Queen,*
Lord Marquess Dorset, [Grey,] Rivers, Hastings,
Catesby, [and] Buckingham.

KING EDWARD

Why, so, now have I done a good day's work.
You peers, continue this united league.
I every day expect an embassage
From my Redeemer to redeem me hence;
And more in peace my soul shall part to heaven,
Since I have made my friends at peace on earth.
Hastings and Rivers, take each other's hand.

8   Dissemble not your hatred, swear your love.

RIVERS

By heaven, my soul is purged from grudging hate,

10 And with my hand I seal my true heart's love.

HASTINGS

11 So thrive I as I truly swear the like.

KING EDWARD

12 Take heed you dally not before your king,
Lest he that is the supreme King of Kings

14 Confound your hidden falsehood and award
Either of you to be the other's end.

HASTINGS

So prosper I as I swear perfect love.

RIVERS

And I as I love Hastings with my heart.

KING EDWARD

Madam, yourself is not exempt from this;
Nor you, son Dorset; Buckingham, nor you:

20 You have been factious one against the other.
Wife, love Lord Hastings, let him kiss your hand,
And what you do, do it unfeignedly.

II.1 The royal palace **s.d.** *Flourish* trumpet call for the king's entrance **8**
Dissemble . . . hatred do not hide hatred under a false appearance (of *love*)
11 *thrive I* may I prosper **12** *dally* trifle **14** *award* cause

QUEEN ELIZABETH
　There, Hastings. I will never more remember
　Our former hatred, so thrive I and mine.　　　　　　　24
KING EDWARD
　Dorset, embrace him; Hastings, love Lord Marquess.
DORSET
　This interchange of love, I here protest,
　Upon my part shall be inviolable.
HASTINGS
　And so swear I. *[They embrace.]*
KING EDWARD
　Now, princely Buckingham, seal thou this league
　With thy embracements to my wife's allies,　　　　　　30
　And make me happy in your unity.
BUCKINGHAM *[To the Queen]*
　Whenever Buckingham doth turn his hate　　　　　　　32
　Upon your grace, but with all duteous love
　Doth cherish you and yours, God punish me
　With hate in those where I expect most love.
　When I have most need to employ a friend,
　And most assurèd that he is a friend,
　Deep, hollow, treacherous, and full of guile
　Be he unto me. This do I beg of God,
　When I am cold in love to you or yours.　　　　　　　40
　　Embrace.
KING EDWARD
　A pleasing cordial, princely Buckingham,　　　　　　　41
　Is this thy vow unto my sickly heart.
　There wanteth now our brother Gloucester here
　To make the blessèd period of this peace.　　　　　　44
　　*Enter [Sir Richard] Ratcliffe and [Richard Duke of]
　　Gloucester.*

---

24 *mine* my family **32–35** *Whenever . . . love* (construction incoherent; for
but, l. 33, understand "nor") **41** *cordial* restorative drink **44** *period* conclusion

BUCKINGHAM
  And in good time,
  Here comes Sir Richard Ratcliffe and the duke.

RICHARD
  Good morrow to my sovereign king and queen;
  And, princely peers, a happy time of day.

KING EDWARD
  Happy indeed, as we have spent the day.
50 Gloucester, we have done deeds of charity,
  Made peace of enmity, fair love of hate,
  Between these swelling wrong-incensèd peers.

RICHARD
  A blessèd labor, my most sovereign lord.
  Among this princely heap, if any here
55 By false intelligence or wrong surmise
  Hold me a foe –
  If I unwittingly, or in my rage,
58 Have aught committed that is hardly borne
  By any in this presence, I desire
60 To reconcile me to his friendly peace.
  'Tis death to me to be at enmity;
  I hate it, and desire all good men's love.
  First, madam, I entreat true peace of you,
  Which I will purchase with my duteous service;
  Of you, my noble cousin Buckingham,
  If ever any grudge were lodged between us;
67 Of you, and you, Lord Rivers, and of Dorset,
68 That, all without desert, have frowned on me;
  Dukes, earls, lords, gentlemen – indeed, of all.
70 I do not know that Englishman alive
  With whom my soul is any jot at odds
  More than the infant that is born tonight.

---

55 *intelligence* information 58 *hardly borne* deeply resented 60 *reconcile . . . peace* bring myself into friendly relations with him 67 *of Dorset*
(*Lord* understood) 68 *all without desert* entirely without my having deserved it

I thank my God for my humility.

QUEEN ELIZABETH
  A holy day shall this be kept hereafter;
  I would to God all strifes were well compounded.   75
  My sovereign lord, I do beseech your highness
  To take our brother Clarence to your grace.

RICHARD
  Why, madam, have I offered love for this,
  To be so flouted in this royal presence?   79
  Who knows not that the gentle duke is dead?   80
    They all start.
  You do him injury to scorn his corpse.   81

KING EDWARD
  Who knows not he is dead? Who knows he is?

QUEEN ELIZABETH
  All-seeing heaven, what a world is this!

BUCKINGHAM
  Look I so pale, Lord Dorset, as the rest?

DORSET
  Ay, my good lord, and no man in the presence   85
  But his red color hath forsook his cheeks.

KING EDWARD
  Is Clarence dead? The order was reversed.

RICHARD
  But he, poor man, by your first order died,
  And that a wingèd Mercury did bear;   89
  Some tardy cripple bore the countermand,   90
  That came too lag to see him burièd.   91
  God grant that some, less noble and less loyal,
  Nearer in bloody thoughts, but not in blood,   93
  Deserve not worse than wretched Clarence did,
  And yet go current from suspicion.   95

---

75 *compounded* resolved 79 *flouted* mocked at 81 *scorn his corpse* i.e., joke
about the dead 85 *presence* i.e., king's presence 89 *Mercury* the quick messenger of the Roman gods 91 *lag* late 93 *in blood* in kinship 95 *go . . .
suspicion* are accepted (as legal tender at face value) without question

Enter [Lord Stanley] Earl of Derby.

DERBY *[Kneeling]*

96   A boon, my sovereign, for my service done.

KING EDWARD

I prithee peace. My soul is full of sorrow.

DERBY

I will not rise unless your highness hear me.

KING EDWARD

Then say at once what is it thou requests.

DERBY

100   The forfeit, sovereign, of my servant's life,

Who slew today a riotous gentleman

Lately attendant on the Duke of Norfolk.

KING EDWARD

Have I a tongue to doom my brother's death,

And shall that tongue give pardon to a slave?

My brother killed no man – his fault was thought –

And yet his punishment was bitter death.

Who sued to me for him? Who, in my wrath,

108   Kneeled at my feet and bid me be advised?

Who spoke of brotherhood? Who spoke of love?

110   Who told me how the poor soul did forsake

111   The mighty Warwick and did fight for me?

Who told me, in the field at Tewkesbury,

113   When Oxford had me down, he rescued me

And said, "Dear brother, live, and be a king"?

Who told me, when we both lay in the field

116   Frozen almost to death, how he did lap me

Even in his garments, and did give himself,

All thin and naked, to the numb-cold night?

All this from my remembrance brutish wrath

120   Sinfully plucked, and not a man of you

Had so much grace to put it in my mind.

---

96 *boon* favor **100** *forfeit . . . life* (the remission of the forfeit is the *boon*)
108 *be advised* take careful thought **111** *Warwick* (Clarence returned to the
Yorkists after marrying Warwick's daughter, thus perjuring himself) **113**
Oxford (an incident neither historical nor in *Henry VI, Part 3*) **116** *lap* wrap

But when your carters or your waiting vassals
Have done a drunken slaughter and defaced
The precious image of our dear Redeemer,
You straight are on your knees for pardon, pardon;   125
And I, unjustly too, must grant it you.
    [Derby rises.]
But for my brother not a man would speak,
Nor I, ungracious, speak unto myself
For him, poor soul. The proudest of you all
Have been beholding to him in his life;   130
Yet none of you would once beg for his life.
O God, I fear thy justice will take hold
On me and you, and mine and yours, for this.
Come, Hastings, help me to my closet. Ah, poor   134
    Clarence!   *Exeunt some with King and Queen.*

RICHARD
This is the fruits of rashness. Marked you not
How that the guilty kindred of the queen
Looked pale when they did hear of Clarence' death?
O, they did urge it still unto the king.
God will revenge it. Come, lords, will you go
To comfort Edward with our company?   140

BUCKINGHAM
We wait upon your grace.   *Exeunt.*

                        *

∽ **II.2** *Enter the old Duchess of York, with the two Chil-
         dren of Clarence [Edward and Margaret Plantagenet].*

BOY
    Good grandam, tell us, is our father dead?

DUCHESS OF YORK No, boy.

GIRL
    Why do you weep so oft, and beat your breast,
    And cry "O Clarence, my unhappy son"?

_____

125 *straight* immediately 134 *closet* private room
    II.2 (No clear textual indication of the setting.)

BOY
> Why do you look on us, and shake your head,
> And call us orphans, wretches, castaways,
> If that our noble father were alive?

DUCHESS OF YORK
8 > My pretty cousins, you mistake me both.
> I do lament the sickness of the king,
10 > As loath to lose him, not your father's death.
> It were lost sorrow to wail one that's lost.

BOY
> Then you conclude, my grandam, he is dead.
> The king mine uncle is to blame for it:
> God will revenge it, whom I will importune
> With earnest prayers all to that effect.

GIRL
> And so will I.

DUCHESS OF YORK
> Peace, children, peace. The king doth love you well.
18 > Incapable and shallow innocents,
> You cannot guess who caused your father's death.

BOY
20 > Grandam, we can, for my good uncle Gloucester
> Told me the king, provoked to it by the queen,
22 > Devised impeachments to imprison him;
> And when my uncle told me so, he wept,
> And pitied me, and kindly kissed my cheek,
> Bade me rely on him as on my father,
> And he would love me dearly as a child.

DUCHESS OF YORK
27 > Ah, that deceit should steal such gentle shape
28 > And with a virtuous visor hide deep vice.
> He is my son – ay, and therein my shame;
30 > Yet from my dugs he drew not this deceit.

---

8 *cousins* kin; *you . . . both* you both misunderstand me 18 *Incapable* without power of understanding 22 *impeachments* accusations 27 *shape* disguise 28 *visor* mask 30 *dugs* breasts

BOY
  Think you my uncle did dissemble, grandam?
DUCHESS OF YORK Ay, boy.
BOY
  I cannot think it. Hark, what noise is this?   33
    Enter the Queen [Elizabeth], with her hair about her
    ears, Rivers and Dorset after her.
QUEEN ELIZABETH
  Ah, who shall hinder me to wail and weep,
  To chide my fortune, and torment myself?
  I'll join with black despair against my soul
  And to myself become an enemy.
DUCHESS OF YORK
  What means this scene of rude impatience?   38
QUEEN ELIZABETH
  To make an act of tragic violence.
  Edward, my lord, thy son, our king, is dead.   40
  Why grow the branches when the root is gone?
  Why wither not the leaves that want their sap?
  If you will live, lament; if die, be brief,
  That our swift-wingèd souls may catch the king's,
  Or like obedient subjects follow him
  To his new kingdom of ne'er-changing night.
DUCHESS OF YORK
  Ah, so much interest have I in thy sorrow
  As I had title in thy noble husband.   48
  I have bewept a worthy husband's death,
  And lived with looking on his images.   50
  But now two mirrors of his princely semblance   51
  Are cracked in pieces by malignant death,
  And I for comfort have but one false glass
  That grieves me when I see my shame in him.

---

33 s.d. *with her . . . ears* (the conventional theatrical sign of extreme grief)
38–39 *scene . . . violence* (note the playhouse imagery; cf. ll. 27–28 and III.5.
1–11) 48 *title* legal right 50 *lived with* i.e., kept myself alive by; *images*
i.e., children 51 *mirrors* i.e., Clarence and King Edward

Thou art a widow, yet thou art a mother,
And hast the comfort of thy children left;
But death hath snatched my husband from mine arms
And plucked two crutches from my feeble hands,
59   Clarence and Edward. O, what cause have I,
60   Thine being but a moiety of my moan,
To overgo thy woes and drown thy cries.

BOY
Ah, aunt, you wept not for our father's death.
63   How can we aid you with our kindred tears?

GIRL
Our fatherless distress was left unmoaned;
Your widow dolor likewise be unwept.

QUEEN ELIZABETH
Give me no help in lamentation.
67   I am not barren to bring forth complaints.
68   All springs reduce their currents to mine eyes,
That I, being governed by the watery moon,
70   May send forth plenteous tears to drown the world.
Ah for my husband, for my dear lord Edward.

CHILDREN
Ah for our father, for our dear lord Clarence.

DUCHESS OF YORK
Alas for both, both mine, Edward and Clarence.

QUEEN ELIZABETH
74   What stay had I but Edward? and he's gone.

CHILDREN
What stay had we but Clarence? and he's gone.

DUCHESS OF YORK
What stays had I but they? and they are gone.

QUEEN ELIZABETH
Was never widow had so dear a loss.

---

59 *what . . . I* what a cause I have 60 *moiety of my moan* half of my grief
63 *kindred tears* i.e., tears belonging to relatives 67 *I . . . complaints* I have
a full capacity for uttering complaints 68 *reduce* bring (as to a reservoir) 74
stay support

CHILDREN
Were never orphans had so dear a loss.

DUCHESS OF YORK
Was never mother had so dear a loss.
Alas, I am the mother of these griefs;   80
Their woes are parceled, mine is general.   81
She for an Edward weeps, and so do I;
I for a Clarence weep, so doth not she;
These babes for Clarence weep, and so do I;
I for an Edward weep, so do not they.
Alas, you three on me, threefold distressed,
Pour all your tears. I am your sorrow's nurse,
And I will pamper it with lamentation.   88

DORSET
Comfort, dear mother. God is much displeased
That you take with unthankfulness his doing.   90
In common worldly things 'tis called ungrateful
With dull unwillingness to repay a debt
Which with a bounteous hand was kindly lent;
Much more to be thus opposite with heaven   94
For it requires the royal debt it lent you.   95

RIVERS
Madam, bethink you like a careful mother
Of the young prince your son. Send straight for him;
Let him be crowned. In him your comfort lives.
Drown desperate sorrow in dead Edward's grave
And plant your joys in living Edward's throne.   100
    Enter Richard, Buckingham, [Stanley Earl of] Derby,
    Hastings, and Ratcliffe.

RICHARD
Sister, have comfort. All of us have cause
To wail the dimming of our shining star,
But none can help our harms by wailing them.
Madam, my mother, I do cry you mercy,

---

81 *parceled* particular to each one 88 *pamper . . . lamentation* i.e., feed sorrow with mourning 94 *opposite with* opposed to 95 *For* because

I did not see your grace. Humbly on my knee
I crave your blessing. *[Kneels.]*

DUCHESS OF YORK
God bless thee, and put meekness in thy breast,
Love, charity, obedience, and true duty.

RICHARD
Amen! – *[Rises; aside]* and make me die a good old man.
110   That is the butt end of a mother's blessing;
I marvel that her grace did leave it out.

BUCKINGHAM
You cloudy princes and heart-sorrowing peers
113   That bear this heavy mutual load of moan,
Now cheer each other in each other's love.
Though we have spent our harvest of this king,
We are to reap the harvest of his son.
117   The broken rancor of your high-swoll'n hates,
118   But lately splintered, knit, and joined together,
Must gently be preserved, cherished, and kept.
120   Me seemeth good that with some little train
121   Forthwith from Ludlow the young prince be fet
Hither to London, to be crowned our king.

RIVERS
Why with some little train, my Lord of Buckingham?

BUCKINGHAM
124   Marry, my lord, lest by a multitude
The new-healed wound of malice should break out,
Which would be so much the more dangerous
127   By how much the estate is green and yet ungoverned.
Where every horse bears his commanding rein
And may direct his course as please himself,

---

110 *butt end* conclusion 113 *load of moan* i.e., weight or cause of lamentation 117–19 *The broken . . . kept* (meaning confused; understand *broken
rancor* as implying "new-found amity") 118 *splintered* set in splints 120
Me seemeth it seems to me 121 *Ludlow* a castle in the town of Ludlow, in
south Shropshire, near the Welsh border (the Prince of Wales was at his royal
residence); *fet* fetched 124 *multitude* large train or following 127 *estate is
green* administration of government is new; *ungoverned* untried

As well the fear of harm as harm apparent,   *130*
In my opinion, ought to be prevented.

RICHARD
I hope the king made peace with all of us,
And the compact is firm and true in me.

RIVERS
And so in me, and so I think in all.
Yet, since it is but green, it should be put
To no apparent likelihood of breach,
Which haply by much company might be urged.   *137*
Therefore I say with noble Buckingham
That it is meet so few should fetch the prince.

HASTINGS
And so say I.   *140*

RICHARD
Then be it so; and go we to determine
Who they shall be that straight shall post to Ludlow.
Madam, and you, my sister, will you go
To give your censures in this business?   *144*

QUEEN ELIZABETH AND DUCHESS OF YORK
With all our hearts.
                    Exeunt. Manent Buckingham and Richard.

BUCKINGHAM
My lord, whoever journeys to the prince,
For God sake let not us two stay at home,
For by the way I'll sort occasion,   *148*
As index to the story we late talked of,   *149*
To part the queen's proud kindred from the prince.   *150*

RICHARD
My other self, my counsel's consistory,   *151*
My oracle, my prophet, my dear cousin,
I, as a child, will go by thy direction.
Toward Ludlow then, for we'll not stay behind. *Exeunt.*
                    *

---

137 *haply* perhaps   144 *censures* judgments   148 *sort occasion* make an
opportunity   149 *index* prologue   151 *consistory* council chamber

∾ **II.3** *Enter one Citizen at one door and another at the other.*

FIRST CITIZEN
  Good morrow, neighbor. Whither away so fast?
SECOND CITIZEN
  I promise you, I scarcely know myself.
  Hear you the news abroad?
FIRST CITIZEN   Yes, that the king is dead.
SECOND CITIZEN
4 Ill news, by'r Lady – seldom comes the better.
5 I fear, I fear 'twill prove a giddy world.
      Enter another Citizen.
THIRD CITIZEN
  Neighbors, God speed.
FIRST CITIZEN   Give you good morrow, sir.
THIRD CITIZEN
  Doth the news hold of good King Edward's death?
SECOND CITIZEN
  Ay, sir, it is too true. God help the while.
THIRD CITIZEN
  Then, masters, look to see a troublous world.
FIRST CITIZEN
10 No, no. By God's good grace his son shall reign.
THIRD CITIZEN
  Woe to that land that's governed by a child.
SECOND CITIZEN
12 In him there is a hope of government,
  Which, in his nonage, council under him,
  And, in his full and ripened years, himself,
  No doubt shall then, and till then, govern well.

II.3 A London street **4** *seldom . . . better* i.e., times are bad but are likely to be worse (proverbial) **5** *giddy* inconstant or mad **12–15** *In him . . . well* (confused construction: there is hope for the land, since one who in his minority governs wisely with the aid of the council will in his maturity govern well in his own person)

FIRST CITIZEN

So stood the state when Henry the Sixth
Was crowned in Paris but at nine months old.

THIRD CITIZEN

Stood the state so? No, no, good friends, God wot,   18
For then this land was famously enriched
With politic grave counsel; then the king   20
Had virtuous uncles to protect his grace.

FIRST CITIZEN

Why, so hath this, both by his father and mother.

THIRD CITIZEN

Better it were they all came by his father,
Or by his father there were none at all,
For emulation who shall now be nearest
Will touch us all too near, if God prevent not.
O, full of danger is the Duke of Gloucester,
And the queen's sons and brothers haught and proud;   28
And were they to be ruled, and not to rule,
This sickly land might solace as before.   30

FIRST CITIZEN

Come, come, we fear the worst. All will be well.

THIRD CITIZEN

When clouds are seen, wise men put on their cloaks;   32
When great leaves fall, then winter is at hand;
When the sun sets, who doth not look for night?
Untimely storms makes men expect a dearth.
All may be well, but if God sort it so,   36
'Tis more than we deserve or I expect.

SECOND CITIZEN

Truly, the hearts of men are full of fear:
You cannot reason almost with a man   39
That looks not heavily and full of dread.   40

---

18 *wot* knows   20 *politic* astute; *counsel* professional advisers   28 *haught* haughty   30 *solace* be happy   32–35 *When . . . dearth* (a series of "moral sentences" in the manner of Senecan tragedy)   36 *sort* dispose   39 *You . . . man* there is almost no man with whom you can reason

THIRD CITIZEN
Before the days of change, still is it so.
By a divine instinct men's minds mistrust
43 Ensuing danger; as by proof we see
The water swell before a boist'rous storm.
But leave it all to God. Whither away?
SECOND CITIZEN
Marry, we were sent for to the justices.
THIRD CITIZEN
And so was I. I'll bear you company.   *Exeunt.*

*

∾ **II.4** *Enter [the] Archbishop [of York], [the] young
[Duke of] York, the Queen [Elizabeth], and the
Duchess [of York].*

ARCHBISHOP
1 Last night, I hear, they lay at Stony Stratford,
2 And at Northampton they do rest tonight.
Tomorrow, or next day, they will be here.
DUCHESS OF YORK
I long with all my heart to see the prince.
I hope he is much grown since last I saw him.
QUEEN ELIZABETH
But I hear no. They say my son of York
Has almost overta'en him in his growth.
YORK
Ay, mother, but I would not have it so.
DUCHESS OF YORK
Why, my good cousin? It is good to grow.
YORK
10 Grandam, one night as we did sit at supper,

---

43 *proof* experience
   II.4 The royal palace 1 *Stony Stratford* a town in Buckinghamshire
2 *Northampton* a town in Northamptonshire (Historically the order of these
two towns is correct, though dramatically the order is difficult, since Stony
Stratford is closer to London than Northampton is – see l. 3. The quartos re-
verse the order.)

My uncle Rivers talked how I did grow
More than my brother. "Ay," quoth my uncle Glouces-
ter,
"Small herbs have grace; great weeds do grow apace."   13
And since, methinks, I would not grow so fast,
Because sweet flow'rs are slow and weeds make haste.

DUCHESS OF YORK
Good faith, good faith, the saying did not hold   16
In him that did object the same to thee.   17
He was the wretched'st thing when he was young,
So long a-growing and so leisurely
That, if his rule were true, he should be gracious.   20

ARCHBISHOP
And so no doubt he is, my gracious madam.

DUCHESS OF YORK
I hope he is, but yet let mothers doubt.

YORK
Now, by my troth, if I had been remembered,   23
I could have given my uncle's grace a flout   24
To touch his growth nearer than he touched mine.

DUCHESS OF YORK
How, my young York? I prithee let me hear it.

YORK
Marry, they say my uncle grew so fast
That he could gnaw a crust at two hours old.
'Twas full two years ere I could get a tooth.
Grandam, this would have been a biting jest.   30

DUCHESS OF YORK
I prithee, pretty York, who told thee this?

YORK
Grandam, his nurse.

DUCHESS OF YORK
His nurse? Why, she was dead ere thou wast born.

---

13 *grace* beneficent virtue; *apace* quickly 16 *hold* hold true 17 *object* urge
20 *gracious* (playing on *grace*, l. 13) 23 *troth* faith; *been remembered* considered 24 *flout* scoff 30 *biting* (note play on "teeth" in ll. 28–29)

YORK
If 'twere not she, I cannot tell who told me.
QUEEN ELIZABETH
35 A parlous boy! Go to, you are too shrewd.
DUCHESS OF YORK
Good madam, be not angry with the child.
QUEEN ELIZABETH
37 Pitchers have ears.
   Enter a Messenger.
ARCHBISHOP
Here comes a messenger. What news?
MESSENGER
Such news, my lord, as grieves me to report.
QUEEN ELIZABETH
40 How doth the prince?
MESSENGER   Well, madam, and in health.
DUCHESS OF YORK
What is thy news?
MESSENGER
42 Lord Rivers and Lord Grey are sent to Pomfret,
43 And with them Sir Thomas Vaughan, prisoners.
DUCHESS OF YORK
Who hath committed them?
MESSENGER   The mighty dukes,
Gloucester and Buckingham.
ARCHBISHOP   For what offense?
MESSENGER
46 The sum of all I can I have disclosed.
Why or for what the nobles were committed
Is all unknown to me, my gracious lord.
QUEEN ELIZABETH
Ay me, I see the ruin of my house.
50 The tiger now hath seized the gentle hind;

---

35 *parlous* cunning 37 *Pitchers have ears* (proverbial: little pitchers have
wide ears – said of children); **s.d.** *Messenger* (in Q the messenger is the
queen's son, the Marquess of Dorset) 42 *Pomfret* Pontefract, a castle in
Yorkshire 43 *Vaughan* (dissyllabic throughout) 46 *can* know

Insulting tyranny begins to jut   51
Upon the innocent and aweless throne.   52
Welcome destruction, blood, and massacre.
I see as in a map the end of all.   54
DUCHESS OF YORK
Accursèd and unquiet wrangling days,
How many of you have mine eyes beheld.
My husband lost his life to get the crown,
And often up and down my sons were tossed
For me to joy and weep their gain and loss;
And being seated, and domestic broils   60
Clean overblown, themselves the conquerors
Make war upon themselves, brother to brother,
Blood to blood, self against self. O preposterous   63
And frantic outrage, end thy damnèd spleen,   64
Or let me die, to look on death no more.
QUEEN ELIZABETH
Come, come, my boy, we will to sanctuary.   66
Madam, farewell.
DUCHESS OF YORK Stay, I will go with you.
QUEEN ELIZABETH
You have no cause.
ARCHBISHOP *[To the Queen]*
                       My gracious lady, go,
And thither bear your treasure and your goods.
For my part, I'll resign unto your grace   70
The seal I keep; and so betide to me   71
As well I tender you and all of yours.   72
Go, I'll conduct you to the sanctuary.   *Exeunt.*
                          *

---

51 *jut* encroach upon **52** *aweless* inspiring no awe **54** *map* (figuratively)
something representing (future) events in epitome **63** *preposterous* inverting
the natural order **64** *spleen* malice **66** *sanctuary* the church precincts in
which civil law was powerless (she goes to Westminster Abbey) **71** *seal* the
stamp used as a sign of authority **72** *tender* care for

❧ **III.1** *The trumpets sound. Enter young Prince [Edward of Wales], the Dukes of Gloucester and Buckingham, Lord Cardinal [Bourchier, Catesby,] with others.*

BUCKINGHAM
1   Welcome, sweet prince, to London, to your chamber.
RICHARD
    Welcome, dear cousin, my thoughts' sovereign:
    The weary way hath made you melancholy.
PRINCE EDWARD
4   No, uncle, but our crosses on the way
    Have made it tedious, wearisome, and heavy.
6   I want more uncles here to welcome me.
RICHARD
    Sweet prince, the untainted virtue of your years
    Hath not yet dived into the world's deceit,
    Nor more can you distinguish of a man
10   Than of his outward show, which, God he knows,
11   Seldom or never jumpeth with the heart.
12   Those uncles which you want were dangerous;
    Your grace attended to their sugared words
    But looked not on the poison of their hearts.
    God keep you from them, and from such false friends.
PRINCE EDWARD
    God keep me from false friends – but they were none.
RICHARD
    My lord, the Mayor of London comes to greet you.
    Enter Lord Mayor [and his train].
LORD MAYOR
    God bless your grace with health and happy days!
PRINCE EDWARD
    I thank you, good my lord, and thank you all.

III.1 A London street 1 *chamber* (London was known as *camera regis*, or
king's chamber) 4 *crosses* annoyances (play on *melancholy*, l. 3) 6 *want* (1)
am lacking in, (2) desire (cf. l. 12) 11 *jumpeth* accords 12 *Those . . . dangerous* (Rivers was Edward's uncle; Grey was his half brother)

I thought my mother and my brother York   20
Would long ere this have met us on the way.
Fie, what a slug is Hastings that he comes not   22
To tell us whether they will come or no!
   Enter Lord Hastings.

BUCKINGHAM
  And, in good time, here comes the sweating lord.

PRINCE EDWARD
  Welcome, my lord. What, will our mother come?

HASTINGS
  On what occasion God he knows, not I,   26
  The queen your mother and your brother York
  Have taken sanctuary. The tender prince
  Would fain have come with me to meet your grace,
  But by his mother was perforce withheld.   30

BUCKINGHAM
  Fie, what an indirect and peevish course   31
  Is this of hers. Lord Cardinal, will your grace
  Persuade the queen to send the Duke of York
  Unto his princely brother presently?   34
  If she deny, Lord Hastings, go with him
  And from her jealous arms pluck him perforce.   36

CARDINAL BOURCHIER
  My Lord of Buckingham, if my weak oratory
  Can from his mother win the Duke of York,
  Anon expect him here, but if she be obdurate
  To mild entreaties, God in heaven forbid   40
  We should infringe the holy privilege
  Of blessèd sanctuary. Not for all this land
  Would I be guilty of so deep a sin.

BUCKINGHAM
  You are too senseless-obstinate, my lord,
  Too ceremonious and traditional.   45

---

22 *slug* lazy fellow (sluggard) 26 *On what occasion* for what reason 30 *perforce* forcibly 31 *indirect and peevish* devious and perverse 34 *presently* at once 36 *jealous* suspicious 45 *ceremonious* tied by formalities

46 Weigh it but with the grossness of this age,
    You break not sanctuary in seizing him;
    The benefit thereof is always granted
    To those whose dealings have deserved the place
50 And those who have the wit to claim the place.
    This prince hath neither claimed it nor deserved it,
    And therefore, in mine opinion, cannot have it.
    Then, taking him from thence that is not there,
    You break no privilege nor charter there.
    Oft have I heard of sanctuary men,
    But sanctuary children never till now.

CARDINAL BOURCHIER
    My lord, you shall overrule my mind for once.
    Come on, Lord Hastings, will you go with me?

HASTINGS
    I go, my lord.

PRINCE EDWARD
60 Good lords, make all the speedy haste you may.
                    Exeunt Cardinal and Hastings.
    Say, uncle Gloucester, if our brother come,
    Where shall we sojourn till our coronation?

RICHARD
    Where it seems best unto your royal self.
    If I may counsel you, some day or two
65 Your highness shall repose you at the Tower;
    Then where you please, and shall be thought most fit
    For your best health and recreation.

PRINCE EDWARD
68 I do not like the Tower, of any place.
    Did Julius Caesar build that place, my lord?

BUCKINGHAM
70 He did, my gracious lord, begin that place,
    Which, since, succeeding ages have re-edified.

---

46 *grossness* coarseness or lack of refinement (in a moral sense) 65 *Tower* the Tower of London (associated in the prince's mind with imprisonment; cf. I.1.45) 68 *of any place* of all places

PRINCE EDWARD
  Is it upon record, or else reported
  Successively from age to age, he built it?
BUCKINGHAM
  Upon record, my gracious lord.
PRINCE EDWARD
  But say, my lord, it were not registered,
  Methinks the truth should live from age to age,
  As 'twere retailed to all posterity,   77
  Even to the general all-ending day.   78
RICHARD *[Aside]*
  So wise so young, they say, do never live long.
PRINCE EDWARD
  What say you, uncle?   80
RICHARD
  I say, without characters fame lives long.   81
    [Aside]
  Thus, like the formal Vice, Iniquity,   82
  I moralize two meanings in one word.   83
PRINCE EDWARD
  That Julius Caesar was a famous man.
  With what his valor did enrich his wit,   85
  His wit set down to make his valor live.
  Death makes no conquest of this conqueror,
  For now he lives in fame, though not in life.
  I'll tell you what, my cousin Buckingham –
BUCKINGHAM
  What, my gracious lord?   90
PRINCE EDWARD
  An if I live until I be a man,   91
  I'll win our ancient right in France again

---

77 *retailed* told 78 *general . . . day* Day of Judgment 81 *characters* written
records 82 *formal Vice, Iniquity* i.e., the conventional Vice figure called Iniquity (the Vice in sixteenth-century morality plays symbolized in one character all the vices) 83 *moralize . . . word* play on a double meaning (as the
Vice did) in a single phrase (i.e., *live long,* l. 79) 85 *what* that with which
91 *An if* if

Or die a soldier as I lived a king.

RICHARD   *[Aside]*

94   Short summers lightly have a forward spring.

> *Enter [the] young [Duke of] York, Hastings, and*
> *Cardinal [Bourchier].*

BUCKINGHAM

Now in good time, here comes the Duke of York.

PRINCE EDWARD

Richard of York, how fares our loving brother?

YORK

97   Well, my dread lord – so must I call you now.

PRINCE EDWARD

Ay, brother – to our grief, as it is yours.

99   Too late he died that might have kept that title,

100   Which by his death hath lost much majesty.

RICHARD

How fares our cousin, noble Lord of York?

YORK

I thank you, gentle uncle. O, my lord,

You said that idle weeds are fast in growth:

The prince my brother hath outgrown me far.

RICHARD

He hath, my lord.

YORK   And therefore is he idle?

RICHARD

O my fair cousin, I must not say so.

YORK

107   Then he is more beholding to you than I.

RICHARD

He may command me as my sovereign,

But you have power in me as in a kinsman.

YORK

110   I pray you, uncle, give me this dagger.

---

94 *Short . . . spring* i.e., those who die young are usually (*lightly*) precocious
(proverbial; cf. l. 79)   97 *dread* to be feared (as king)   99 *late* recently   107
beholding indebted

RICHARD

    My dagger, little cousin? With all my heart.   111

PRINCE EDWARD

    A beggar, brother?

YORK

    Of my kind uncle, that I know will give,

    And being but a toy, which is no grief to give.

RICHARD

    A greater gift than that I'll give my cousin.

YORK

    A greater gift? O, that's the sword to it.

RICHARD

    Ay, gentle cousin, were it light enough.

YORK

    O, then I see you will part but with light gifts!   118

    In weightier things you'll say a beggar nay.

RICHARD

    It is too heavy for your grace to wear.   *120*

YORK

    I weigh it lightly, were it heavier.   *121*

RICHARD

    What, would you have my weapon, little lord?

YORK

    I would, that I might thank you as you call me.

RICHARD How?

YORK Little.

PRINCE EDWARD

    My Lord of York will still be cross in talk.   126

    Uncle, your grace knows how to bear with him.

YORK

    You mean, to bear me, not to bear with me.

    Uncle, my brother mocks both you and me:

---

111 *My . . . heart* (Richard would, with all his heart, like to give York his
dagger in his heart) 118 *light* slight or trivial 121 *weigh it lightly* consider
it of little value 126 *still be cross* always be opposite, contrary

130   Because that I am little, like an ape,
    He thinks that you should bear me on your shoulders.

BUCKINGHAM   *[Aside to Hastings]*
132   With what a sharp-provided wit he reasons.
    To mitigate the scorn he gives his uncle,
    He prettily and aptly taunts himself.
    So cunning, and so young, is wonderful.

RICHARD
    My lord, will't please you pass along?
    Myself and my good cousin Buckingham
    Will to your mother, to entreat of her
    To meet you at the Tower and welcome you.

YORK
140   What, will you go unto the Tower, my lord?

PRINCE EDWARD
    My Lord Protector needs will have it so.

YORK
    I shall not sleep in quiet at the Tower.

RICHARD
    Why, what should you fear?

YORK
    Marry, my uncle Clarence' angry ghost:
    My grandam told me he was murdered there.

PRINCE EDWARD
    I fear no uncles dead.

RICHARD
    Nor none that live, I hope.

PRINCE EDWARD
148   An if they live, I hope I need not fear.
    But come, my lord; and with a heavy heart,
150   Thinking on them, go I unto the Tower.
    A sennet. Exeunt Prince [Edward], York, Hastings
    [,Cardinal Bourchier, and others]. Manent Richard,
    Buckingham, and Catesby.

130–31 *Because . . . shoulders* (alluding to jesters and bears carrying monkeys at fairs – and hence to Richard's hunchback) 132 *sharp-provided* keenly thought out 148 *they* i.e., Rivers and Grey 150 s.d. *sennet* trumpet call for a procession

BUCKINGHAM

Think you, my lord, this little prating York   151
Was not incensèd by his subtle mother   152
To taunt and scorn you thus opprobriously?

RICHARD

No doubt, no doubt. O, 'tis a perilous boy,   154
Bold, quick, ingenious, forward, capable:
He is all the mother's, from the top to toe.   156

BUCKINGHAM

Well, let them rest. Come hither, Catesby.   157
Thou art sworn as deeply to effect what we intend
As closely to conceal what we impart.
Thou know'st our reasons urged upon the way.   160
What think'st thou? Is it not an easy matter
To make William Lord Hastings of our mind
For the installment of this noble duke   163
In the seat royal of this famous isle?

CATESBY

He for his father's sake so loves the prince   165
That he will not be won to aught against him.

BUCKINGHAM

What think'st thou then of Stanley? Will not he?   167

CATESBY

He will do all in all as Hastings doth.

BUCKINGHAM

Well then, no more but this: go, gentle Catesby,
And, as it were far off, sound thou Lord Hastings   170
How he doth stand affected to our purpose,   171
And summon him tomorrow to the Tower
To sit about the coronation.   173

---

151 *prating* overtalkative 152 *incensèd* incited 154 *perilous* shrewd or dangerously cunning (cf. *parlous*, II.4.35, the more usual form, but Richard's use of the stronger form may here be intentional) 156 *He . . . mother's* i.e., he takes after his mother 157 *let them rest* i.e., leave them (for the moment) 163 *installment* formal installation 165 *his* i.e., the prince's 167 *Stanley* i.e., the Earl of Derby, Lord Stanley 171 *How . . . affected* how he is disposed 173 *sit* i.e., hold consultation

174　　If thou dost find him tractable to us,
　　　　Encourage him, and tell him all our reasons.
　　　　If he be leaden, icy, cold, unwilling,
　　　　Be thou so too, and so break off the talk,
　　　　And give us notice of his inclination,
179　　For we tomorrow hold divided councils,
180　　Wherein thyself shalt highly be employed.

RICHARD

181　　Commend me to Lord William. Tell him, Catesby,
　　　　His ancient knot of dangerous adversaries
　　　　Tomorrow are let blood at Pomfret Castle,
　　　　And bid my lord, for joy of this good news,
　　　　Give Mistress Shore one gentle kiss the more.

BUCKINGHAM

　　　　Good Catesby, go effect this business soundly.

CATESBY

　　　　My good lords both, with all the heed I can.

RICHARD

　　　　Shall we hear from you, Catesby, ere we sleep?

CATESBY

　　　　You shall, my lord.

RICHARD

190　　At Crosby House, there shall you find us both.

Exit Catesby.

BUCKINGHAM

　　　　Now, my lord, what shall we do if we perceive
192　　Lord Hastings will not yield to our complots?

RICHARD

　　　　Chop off his head. Something we will determine.
194　　And look when I am king, claim thou of me
195　　The earldom of Hereford and all the movables
　　　　Whereof the king my brother was possessed.

---

174 *tractable* compliant　179 *divided councils* i.e., two separate council meetings (cf. III.2.12–14), one a private consultation unknown to the public council　181 *Lord William* i.e., Hastings　192 *complots* conspiracies 194 *look when* as soon as　195 *movables* (cf. Holinshed: "a great quantitie of the kings treasure, and of his household stuffe")

BUCKINGHAM
  I'll claim that promise at your grace's hand.
RICHARD
  And look to have it yielded with all kindness.
  Come, let us sup betimes, that afterwards   199
  We may digest our complots in some form.   *Exeunt.*   200

                          *

❧ **III.2** *Enter a Messenger to the door of [Lord] Hastings.*

MESSENGER
  My lord, my lord!
HASTINGS *[Within]*
  Who knocks?
MESSENGER
  One from the Lord Stanley.
    Enter Lord Hastings.
HASTINGS
  What is't o'clock?
MESSENGER
  Upon the stroke of four.
HASTINGS
  Cannot my Lord Stanley sleep these tedious nights?   6
MESSENGER
  So it appears by that I have to say:
  First, he commends him to your noble self.
HASTINGS
  What then?
MESSENGER
  Then certifies your lordship that this night   10
  He dreamt the boar had razèd off his helm.   11
  Besides, he says there are two councils kept;

―――――――――
199 *betimes* early
  III.2 Lord Hastings' house 6 *tedious* (this word seems to suggest that
Hastings cannot sleep either) 11 *boar* (Richard's symbol; see I.3.228);
razèd . . . helm i.e., cut off his head

And that may be determined at the one
14 Which may make you and him to rue at th' other.
Therefore he sends to know your lordship's pleasure,
16 If you will presently take horse with him
And with all speed post with him toward the north
18 To shun the danger that his soul divines.

HASTINGS
Go, fellow, go, return unto thy lord.
20 Bid him not fear the separated council.
His honor and myself are at the one,
And at the other is my good friend Catesby,
Where nothing can proceed that toucheth us
Whereof I shall not have intelligence.
25 Tell him his fears are shallow, without instance;
26 And for his dreams, I wonder he's so simple
To trust the mock'ry of unquiet slumbers.
To fly the boar before the boar pursues
Were to incense the boar to follow us,
30 And make pursuit where he did mean no chase.
Go, bid thy master rise and come to me,
And we will both together to the Tower,
Where he shall see the boar will use us kindly.

MESSENGER
I'll go, my lord, and tell him what you say.   *Exit.*
    Enter Catesby.

CATESBY
Many good morrows to my noble lord.

HASTINGS
Good morrow, Catesby. You are early stirring.
What news, what news, in this our tott'ring state?

CATESBY
38 It is a reeling world indeed, my lord,
And I believe will never stand upright
40 Till Richard wear the garland of the realm.

---

14 *rue* grieve (at what was decided) 16 *presently* at once 18 *divines* perceives 25 *instance* evidence 26 *simple* foolish 38 *reeling* (cf. II.3.5)

HASTINGS
  How? wear the garland? Doest thou mean the crown?
CATESBY
  Ay, my good lord.
HASTINGS
  I'll have this crown of mine cut from my shoulders   43
  Before I'll see the crown so foul misplaced.
  But canst thou guess that he doth aim at it?
CATESBY
  Ay, on my life, and hopes to find you forward   46
  Upon his party for the gain thereof;
  And thereupon he sends you this good news,
  That this same very day your enemies,
  The kindred of the queen, must die at Pomfret.   50
HASTINGS
  Indeed I am no mourner for that news,
  Because they have been still my adversaries;   52
  But that I'll give my voice on Richard's side
  To bar my master's heirs in true descent –
  God knows I will not do it, to the death.
CATESBY
  God keep your lordship in that gracious mind.
HASTINGS
  But I shall laugh at this a twelvemonth hence,   57
  That they which brought me in my master's hate,
  I live to look upon their tragedy.
  Well, Catesby, ere a fortnight make me older,   60
  I'll send some packing that yet think not on't.
CATESBY
  'Tis a vile thing to die, my gracious lord,
  When men are unprepared and look not for it.

---

43 *crown . . . shoulders* (foreshadows Hastings' death and looks back to l.
11) 46–47 *forward / Upon* lending strong support to 52 *still* always 57–59
But . . . tragedy (construction difficult; for the sense, omit *they* in l. 58 and
insert l. 59 after *That* in l. 58)

HASTINGS
    O monstrous, monstrous! And so falls it out
    With Rivers, Vaughan, Grey; and so 'twill do
    With some men else, that think themselves as safe
    As thou and I, who, as thou know'st, are dear
    To princely Richard and to Buckingham.
CATESBY
    The princes both make high account of you –
    [Aside]
70   For they account his head upon the Bridge.
HASTINGS
    I know they do, and I have well deserved it.
    Enter Lord Stanley [Earl of Derby].
72   Come on, come on! Where is your boar spear, man?
    Fear you the boar, and go so unprovided?
DERBY
    My lord, good morrow. Good morrow, Catesby.
75   You may jest on, but, by the Holy Rood,
    I do not like these several councils, I.
HASTINGS
    My lord,
    I hold my life as dear as you do yours,
    And never in my days, I do protest,
80   Was it so precious to me as 'tis now.
    Think you, but that I know our state secure,
82   I would be so triumphant as I am?
DERBY
    The lords at Pomfret, when they rode from London,
84   Were jocund and supposed their states were sure,
    And they indeed had no cause to mistrust;
    But yet you see how soon the day o'ercast.
87   This sudden stab of rancor I misdoubt:
    Pray God, I say, I prove a needless coward.

---

70 *account* expect; *Bridge* London Bridge (traitors' heads were displayed on poles on its gateway entrances) 72 *boar spear* spear with a crossbar for hunting boar 75 *Holy Rood* Christ's cross 82 *triumphant* exultant 84 *jocund* merry 87 *This . . . misdoubt* i.e., I fear this sudden blow (the capture of Rivers, Vaughan, and Grey) arising out of hatred

What, shall we toward the Tower? The day is spent.

HASTINGS
Come, come, have with you. Wot you what, my lord?   90
Today the lords you talked of are beheaded.

DERBY
They, for their truth, might better wear their heads
Than some that have accused them wear their hats.   93
But come, my lord, let's away.   94
    Enter a Pursuivant [also named Hastings].

HASTINGS
Go on before. I'll talk with this good fellow.
        Exeunt Lord Stanley [Earl of Derby], and Catesby.
How now, sirrah? How goes the world with thee?

PURSUIVANT
The better that your lordship please to ask.

HASTINGS
I tell thee, man, 'tis better with me now
Than when thou met'st me last where now we meet.
Then was I going prisoner to the Tower   100
By the suggestion of the queen's allies.
But now I tell thee, keep it to thyself,
This day those enemies are put to death,
And I in better state than e'er I was.

PURSUIVANT
God hold it, to your honor's good content.   105

HASTINGS
Gramercy, fellow. There, drink that for me.   106
    Throws him his purse.

PURSUIVANT   I thank your honor.   *Exit Pursuivant.*
    Enter a Priest.

PRIEST
Well met, my lord. I am glad to see your honor.

---

93 *some . . . hats* (probably a veiled reference to Richard and Buckingham,
whose rank as dukes gave them the privilege of wearing the so-called ducal
cap in the royal presence, no head covering resembling a hat being allowed
below the rank of duke) 94 **s.d.** *Pursuivant* state messenger with authority
to execute warrants 105 *God hold it* i.e., may God continue this state of affairs 106 *Gramercy* much thanks

HASTINGS

109 I thank thee, good Sir John, with all my heart.

110 I am in your debt for your last exercise;
Come the next Sabbath, and I will content you.

PRIEST

I'll wait upon your lordship.
Enter Buckingham.

BUCKINGHAM

What, talking with a priest, Lord Chamberlain?
Your friends at Pomfret, they do need the priest;

115 Your honor hath no shriving work in hand.

HASTINGS

Good faith, and when I met this holy man,
The men you talk of came into my mind.
What, go you toward the Tower?

BUCKINGHAM

I do, my lord, but long I cannot stay there.

120 I shall return before your lordship thence.

HASTINGS

121 Nay, like enough, for I stay dinner there.

BUCKINGHAM *[Aside]*

And supper too, although thou know'st it not. —
Come, will you go?

HASTINGS   I'll wait upon your lordship. *Exeunt.*

*

∽ III.3 *Enter Sir Richard Ratcliffe, with Halberds,
carrying the Nobles [Rivers, Grey, and Vaughan]
to death at Pomfret.*

RATCLIFFE Come, bring forth the prisoners.

---

109 *Sir John* ("sir" was a title of respect applied to the clergy; no reference
here to knighthood)   110 *exercise* sermon   115 *shriving work* i.e.,
"deathbed" confessions   121 *stay* stay for; *dinner* (eaten in late morning)
    III.3 Pontefract Castle (called Pomfret in the play) s.d. *Halberds* men
carrying halberds (a combination spear and ax)

RIVERS
Sir Richard Ratcliffe, let me tell thee this:
Today shalt thou behold a subject die
For truth, for duty, and for loyalty.

GREY
God bless the prince from all the pack of you!
A knot you are of damnèd bloodsuckers.   6

VAUGHAN
You live that shall cry woe for this hereafter.

RATCLIFFE
Dispatch. The limit of your lives is out.

RIVERS
O Pomfret, Pomfret! O thou bloody prison,
Fatal and ominous to noble peers!   10
Within the guilty closure of thy walls
Richard the Second here was hacked to death;
And, for more slander to thy dismal seat,   13
We give to thee our guiltless blood to drink.

GREY
Now Margaret's curse is fall'n upon our heads,   15
When she exclaimed on Hastings, you, and I,
For standing by when Richard stabbed her son.

RIVERS
Then cursed she Richard, then cursed she Bucking-
    ham,
Then cursed she Hastings. O, remember, God,
To hear her prayer for them, as now for us.   20
And for my sister and her princely sons,
Be satisfied, dear God, with our true blood,
Which, as thou know'st, unjustly must be spilt.

RATCLIFFE
Make haste. The hour of death is expiate.   24

---

6 *knot* patch 13 *for . . . seat* i.e., in order to bring greater shame upon *Pom-fret*, a place that already bodes disaster 15–19 *Now . . . Hastings* (this is not an accurate account of the curses in I.3, but Shakespeare appears not to worry about such details) 24 *expiate* fully come (cf. l. 8)

RIVERS
    Come, Grey; come, Vaughan; let us here embrace.
    Farewell, until we meet again in heaven.   *Exeunt.*
                                    *

❧ **III.4** *Enter Buckingham, [Lord Stanley Earl of]*
    Derby, Hastings, Bishop of Ely, Norfolk, Ratcliffe,
    Lovel, with others, at a table.

HASTINGS
    Now, noble peers, the cause why we are met
2   Is to determine of the coronation.
    In God's name, speak. When is the royal day?
BUCKINGHAM
    Is all things ready for the royal time?
DERBY
5   It is, and wants but nomination.
BISHOP OF ELY
    Tomorrow then I judge a happy day.
BUCKINGHAM
    Who knows the Lord Protector's mind herein?
8   Who is most inward with the noble duke?
BISHOP OF ELY
    Your grace, we think, should soonest know his mind.
BUCKINGHAM
10 We know each other's faces; for our hearts,
    He knows no more of mine than I of yours,
    Or I of his, my lord, than you of mine.
    Lord Hastings, you and he are near in love.
HASTINGS
    I thank his grace, I know he loves me well;
    But, for his purpose in the coronation,

III.4 The Tower of London **s.d.** *Ratcliffe, Lovel* (Ratcliffe had been at Ponte-fract [Pomfret] in III.3; Q replaces both with Catesby) **2** *determine of* come to a decision concerning **5** *nomination* naming the day **8** *inward* intimate **10** *for* as for

I have not sounded him, nor he delivered   16
His gracious pleasure any way therein.
But you, my honorable lords, may name the time,
And in the duke's behalf I'll give my voice,
Which, I presume, he'll take in gentle part.   20
   Enter [Richard Duke of] Gloucester.

BISHOP OF ELY
In happy time, here comes the duke himself.

RICHARD
My noble lords and cousins all, good morrow.
I have been long a sleeper, but I trust
My absence doth neglect no great design   24
Which by my presence might have been concluded.

BUCKINGHAM
Had you not come upon your cue, my lord,
William Lord Hastings had pronounced your part –
I mean, your voice for crowning of the king.

RICHARD
Than my Lord Hastings no man might be bolder.
His lordship knows me well, and loves me well.   30
My Lord of Ely, when I was last in Holborn   31
I saw good strawberries in your garden there.
I do beseech you send for some of them.

BISHOP OF ELY
Marry and will, my lord, with all my heart.
                     Exit Bishop.

RICHARD
Cousin of Buckingham, a word with you.
   [Takes him aside.]
Catesby hath sounded Hastings in our business
And finds the testy gentleman so hot   37
That he will lose his head ere give consent

---

16 *I . . . him* (but Richard had in fact *sounded Hastings;* cf. l. 36) 24 *neglect . . . design* i.e., cause no great design to be neglected 31 *Holborn* (area of London where the Bishop of Ely's palace was) 37 *testy* quick-tempered; *hot* burning (with his resolve)

39   His master's child, as worshipfully he terms it,
40   Shall lose the royalty of England's throne.
BUCKINGHAM
    Withdraw yourself awhile. I'll go with you.
                    Exeunt [Richard and Buckingham].
DERBY
    We have not yet set down this day of triumph:
    Tomorrow, in my judgment, is too sudden,
    For I myself am not so well provided
45   As else I would be, were the day prolonged.
        Enter the Bishop of Ely.
BISHOP OF ELY
    Where is my lord the Duke of Gloucester?
    I have sent for these strawberries.
HASTINGS
    His grace looks cheerfully and smooth this morning;
49   There's some conceit or other likes him well
50   When that he bids good morrow with such spirit.
    I think there's never a man in Christendom
    Can lesser hide his love or hate than he,
    For by his face straight shall you know his heart.
DERBY
    What of his heart perceive you in his face
55   By any livelihood he showed today?
HASTINGS
    Marry, that with no man here he is offended;
    For were he, he had shown it in his looks.
DERBY
    I pray God he be not, I say.
        Enter Richard and Buckingham.
RICHARD
    I pray you all, tell me what they deserve
60   That do conspire my death with devilish plots

---

39 *worshipfully* i.e., using words expressing honor or regard **40** *royalty* sovereignty **45** *the day prolonged* i.e., a later day set **49** *conceit* (happy) idea or device **55** *livelihood* vivacity

Of damnèd witchcraft, and that have prevailed   61
Upon my body with their hellish charms.

HASTINGS
The tender love I bear your grace, my lord,
Makes me most forward in this princely presence
To doom th' offenders, whosoe'er they be.
I say, my lord, they have deservèd death.

RICHARD
Then be your eyes the witness of their evil.
Look how I am bewitched. Behold, mine arm
Is like a blasted sapling, withered up;
And this is Edward's wife, that monstrous witch,   70
Consorted with that harlot, strumpet Shore,   71
That by their witchcraft thus have markèd me.

HASTINGS
If they have done this deed, my noble lord –

RICHARD
If? Thou protector of this damnèd strumpet,
Talk'st thou to me of ifs? Thou art a traitor.
Off with his head! Now by Saint Paul I swear
I will not dine until I see the same.
Lovel and Ratcliffe, look that it be done.
The rest that love me, rise and follow me.

                    Exeunt. Manent Lovel and Ratcliffe,
                              with the Lord Hastings.

HASTINGS
Woe, woe for England, not a whit for me,   80
For I, too fond, might have prevented this.   81
Stanley did dream the boar did raze our helms;
But I did scorn it and disdain to fly.
Three times today my footcloth horse did stumble,   84
And started when he looked upon the Tower,
As loath to bear me to the slaughterhouse.

61–62 *prevailed / Upon* got the better of   71 *Consorted* associated   80 *whit*
bit   81 *fond* foolish   84 *footcloth horse* horse caparisoned with a richly
wrought covering reaching almost to the ground

O, now I need the priest that spake to me.
I now repent I told the pursuivant,
89 As too triumphing, how mine enemies
90 Today at Pomfret bloodily were butchered,
And I myself secure, in grace and favor.
O Margaret, Margaret, now thy heavy curse
Is lighted on poor Hastings' wretched head.

RATCLIFFE
Come, come, dispatch. The duke would be at dinner.
95 Make a short shrift; he longs to see your head.

HASTINGS
96 O momentary grace of mortal men,
Which we more hunt for than the grace of God.
98 Who builds his hope in air of your good looks
Lives like a drunken sailor on a mast,
100 Ready with every nod to tumble down
Into the fatal bowels of the deep.

LOVEL
102 Come, come, dispatch. 'Tis bootless to exclaim.

HASTINGS
O bloody Richard! Miserable England,
I prophesy the fearfull'st time to thee
That ever wretched age hath looked upon.
Come, lead me to the block; bear him my head.
They smile at me who shortly shall be dead.   *Exeunt.*

*

∾ **III.5** *Enter Richard [Duke of Gloucester], and*
Buckingham, in rotten armor, marvelous ill-favored.

RICHARD
Come, cousin, canst thou quake and change thy color,
Murder thy breath in middle of a word,

---

89 *triumphing* exulting 95 *shrift* religious confession 96 *grace* favor 98
of . . . looks out of your kind glances (suggesting approval) 102 *bootless* useless
    III.5 (No clear textual indication of the setting.) **s.d.** *rotten* rusty; *ill-*
favored ugly

And then again begin, and stop again,
As if thou were distraught and mad with terror?
BUCKINGHAM
    Tut, I can counterfeit the deep tragedian,
    Speak and look back, and pry on every side,
    Tremble and start at wagging of a straw,   7
    Intending deep suspicion, ghastly looks   8
    Are at my service, like enforcèd smiles,
    And both are ready in their offices,   10
    At any time to grace my stratagems.
    But what, is Catesby gone?
RICHARD
    He is, and see, he brings the mayor along.
        Enter the Mayor and Catesby.
BUCKINGHAM
    Lord Mayor –
RICHARD
    Look to the drawbridge there!
BUCKINGHAM
    Hark, a drum!
RICHARD
    Catesby, o'erlook the walls.   17
BUCKINGHAM
    Lord Mayor, the reason we have sent –
        Enter Lovel and Ratcliffe, with Hastings' head.
RICHARD
    Look back, defend thee! Here are enemies!
BUCKINGHAM
    God and our innocence defend and guard us.   20
RICHARD
    Be patient, they are friends, Ratcliffe and Lovel.
LOVEL
    Here is the head of that ignoble traitor,
    The dangerous and unsuspected Hastings.

---

7 *wagging of a straw* the least movement 8 *Intending* pretending 10 *offices*
particular functions 17 *o'erlook* look out over

RICHARD

 So dear I loved the man that I must weep.
25 I took him for the plainest harmless creature
 That breathed upon the earth a Christian;
27 Made him my book, wherein my soul recorded
 The history of all her secret thoughts.
 So smooth he daubed his vice with show of virtue
30 That, his apparent open guilt omitted –
31 I mean, his conversation with Shore's wife –
32 He lived from all attainder of suspects.

BUCKINGHAM

33 Well, well, he was the covert'st sheltered traitor
 That ever lived.
 Would you imagine, or almost believe,
36 Were't not that by great preservation
 We live to tell it, that the subtle traitor
 This day had plotted, in the Council House,
 To murder me and my good Lord of Gloucester?

MAYOR

40 Had he done so?

RICHARD

 What? Think you we are Turks or infidels?
 Or that we would, against the form of law,
 Proceed thus rashly in the villain's death
 But that the extreme peril of the case,
 The peace of England, and our persons' safety
 Enforced us to this execution?

MAYOR

 Now fair befall you. He deserved his death,
48 And your good graces both have well proceeded
 To warn false traitors from the like attempts.

BUCKINGHAM

50 I never looked for better at his hands

---

25 *harmless* (supply "most"; cf. l. 33) 27 *book* i.e., table book, or diary 31 *conversation* (sexual) intercourse 32 *attainder of suspects* stain of suspicions 33 *sheltered* hidden (supply "most") 36 *great preservation* i.e., the fortunate forestalling of an evil that might have happened 48 *proceeded* done

After he once fell in with Mistress Shore.
Yet had we not determined he should die
Until your lordship came to see his end,
Which now the loving haste of these our friends,
Something against our meanings, have prevented,   55
Because, my lord, I would have had you heard
The traitor speak, and timorously confess   57
The manner and the purpose of his treasons,
That you might well have signified the same
Unto the citizens, who haply may   60
Misconster us in him and wail his death.   61

MAYOR
But, my good lord, your grace's words shall serve,
As well as I had seen, and heard him speak;
And do not doubt, right noble princes both,
But I'll acquaint our duteous citizens
With all your just proceedings in this cause.   66

RICHARD
And to that end we wished your lordship here,
T' avoid the censures of the carping world.   68

BUCKINGHAM
But since you come too late of our intent,   69
Yet witness what you hear we did intend;   70
And so, my good Lord Mayor, we bid farewell.
                                            Exit Mayor.

RICHARD
Go after, after, cousin Buckingham.
The mayor towards Guildhall hies him in all post.   73
There, at your meetest vantage of the time,   74
Infer the bastardy of Edward's children.
Tell them how Edward put to death a citizen
Only for saying he would make his son

---

55 *prevented* anticipated 57 *timorously* full of fear 60 *haply* perhaps 61
Misconster . . . him i.e., misunderstand our manner of dealing with him 66
cause affair or action (perhaps with legal overtones) 68 *carping* overcritical
69 *of* i.e., in terms of 70 *witness* i.e., bear witness to 73 *Guildhall* the
"town hall" of London; *post* haste 74 *meetest . . . time* i.e., the most advan-
tageous moment

78 Heir to the Crown, meaning indeed his house,
    Which by the sign thereof was termèd so.
80 Moreover, urge his hateful luxury
81 And bestial appetite in change of lust,
    Which stretched unto their servants, daughters, wives,
    Even where his raging eye or savage heart,
    Without control, lusted to make a prey.
    Nay, for a need, thus far come near my person:
    Tell them, when that my mother went with child
    Of that insatiate Edward, noble York,
    My princely father, then had wars in France,
    And by true computation of the time
90 Found that the issue was not his begot,
91 Which well appearèd in his lineaments,
    Being nothing like the noble duke my father.
    Yet touch this sparingly, as 'twere far off,
    Because, my lord, you know my mother lives.

BUCKINGHAM
    Doubt not, my lord, I'll play the orator
96 As if the golden fee for which I plead
    Were for myself – and so, my lord, adieu.

RICHARD
98 If you thrive well, bring them to Baynard's Castle,
    Where you shall find me well accompanied
100 With reverend fathers and well-learnèd bishops.

BUCKINGHAM
    I go, and towards three or four o'clock
    Look for the news that the Guildhall affords.
                                        Exit Buckingham.

RICHARD
103 Go, Lovel, with all speed to Doctor Shaw –
    [To Catesby]

---

78 *Crown . . . house* i.e., a tavern called The Crown 80 *luxury* lasciviousness
81 *change of lust* i.e., alteration in the object of his lust 90 *issue* offspring
91 *lineaments* appearance 96 *golden fee* i.e., the crown (play on "lawyer's
fee") 98 *Baynard's Castle* (Richard's stronghold between Blackfriars and
London Bridge) 103 *Shaw* (brother to the Lord Mayor); **s.d.** (Richard
could be speaking to either Catesby or Ratcliffe)

Go thou to Friar Penker. – Bid them both   104
Meet me within this hour at Baynard's Castle.
                    Exeunt [Lovel, Catesby, and Ratcliffe].
Now will I go to take some privy order   106
To draw the brats of Clarence out of sight,
And to give order that no manner person   108
Have any time recourse unto the princes.   *Exit.*

                    ✳

❧ **III.6** *Enter a Scrivener [with a paper in his hand].*

SCRIVENER
Here is the indictment of the good Lord Hastings,
Which in a set hand fairly is engrossed   2
That it may be today read o'er in Paul's.   3
And mark how well the sequel hangs together:
Eleven hours I have spent to write it over,
For yesternight by Catesby was it sent me;
The precedent was full as long a-doing,   7
And yet within these five hours Hastings lived,
Untainted, unexamined, free, at liberty.   9
Here's a good world the while! Who is so gross   10
That cannot see this palpable device?
Yet who so bold but says he sees it not?
Bad is the world, and all will come to naught   13
When such ill dealing must be seen in thought.   *Exit.*   14

                    ✳

---

104 *Penker* (Friar Perkins, provincial of the Augustinian order and, like Shaw, a preacher who gave sermons in praise of Richard)   106 *take . . . order* make some secret arrangement   108–9 *no . . . unto* i.e., no person of any sort should have, at any time, admittance to

   III.6 London   2 *in . . . engrossed* is written neatly in a formal legal hand   3 *Paul's* Saint Paul's Cathedral   7 *precedent* exemplar (i.e., the prepared indictment)   9 *Untainted* unaccused   10 *the while* just now; *gross* stupid   13 *naught* evil   14 *seen in thought* expressed only in thinking

◌ **III.7** *Enter Richard [Duke of Gloucester] and*
Buckingham at several doors.

RICHARD
How now, how now? What say the citizens?
BUCKINGHAM
Now, by the holy Mother of our Lord,
The citizens are mum, say not a word.
RICHARD
Touched you the bastardy of Edward's children?
BUCKINGHAM

5 I did, with his contract with Lady Lucy
6 And his contract by deputy in France,
   Th' unsatiate greediness of his desire
8 And his enforcement of the city wives,
   His tyranny for trifles, his own bastardy,
10 As being got, your father then in France,
   And his resemblance, being not like the duke.
   Withal I did infer your lineaments,
13 Being the right idea of your father
   Both in your form and nobleness of mind,
15 Laid open all your victories in Scotland,
   Your discipline in war, wisdom in peace,
   Your bounty, virtue, fair humility,
   Indeed, left nothing fitting for your purpose
19 Untouched, or slightly handled in discourse;
20 And when mine oratory drew to an end,
   I bid them that did love their country's good
   Cry, "God save Richard, England's royal king!"

III.7 Baynard's Castle **5** *Lady Lucy* Elizabeth Lucy (to whom Edward IV
was not actually contracted, although she bore him a child) **6** *contract . . .
France* (reference to Edward IV's overtures for marriage with Bona, sister-in-
law of Lewis IX of France; cf. *Henry VI, Part 3*, III.3, and below, ll. 181–82;
Edward's precontract with these two women might be held to invalidate his
marriage to Elizabeth) **8** *enforcement* rape **10** *got* begot, conceived **13**
right idea true image **15** *your victories in Scotland* (Richard's expedition in
1482 had advanced as far as Edinburgh) **19** *slightly handled* lightly touched on

RICHARD
  And did they so?
BUCKINGHAM
  No, so God help me, they spake not a word,
  But, like dumb statuës or breathing stones,   25
  Stared each on other, and looked deadly pale.
  Which when I saw, I reprehended them
  And asked the mayor what meant this willful silence.
  His answer was, the people were not used
  To be spoke to but by the recorder.   30
  Then he was urged to tell my tale again:
  "Thus saith the duke, thus hath the duke inferred" –
  But nothing spoke in warrant from himself.
  When he had done, some followers of mine own,
  At lower end of the hall, hurled up their caps,
  And some ten voices cried, "God save King Richard!"
  And thus I took the vantage of those few: 37
  "Thanks, gentle citizens and friends," quoth I.
  "This general applause and cheerful shout
  Argues your wisdoms and your love to Richard" –   40
  And even here brake off and came away.
RICHARD
  What tongueless blocks were they! Would they not
    speak?
BUCKINGHAM
  No, by my troth, my lord.
RICHARD
  Will not the mayor then and his brethren come?
BUCKINGHAM
  The mayor is here at hand. Intend some fear,   45
  Be not you spoke with but by mighty suit,   46
  And look you get a prayer book in your hand
  And stand between two churchmen, good my lord,

---

25 *statuës* (trisyllabic) **30** *recorder* (magistrate appointed by the mayor and aldermen to serve as an "oral record" of proceedings in city law courts and government) **37** *vantage* opportunity **45** *Intend* pretend **46** *by mighty suit* by great solicitation

49 For on that ground I'll make a holy descant,
50 And be not easily won to our requests.
51 Play the maid's part: still answer nay, and take it.
RICHARD
    I go; and if you plead as well for them
    As I can say nay to thee for myself,
    No doubt we bring it to a happy issue.
BUCKINGHAM
55 Go, go, up to the leads! The Lord Mayor knocks.
                                    [Exit Richard.]
    Enter the Mayor [, Aldermen,] and Citizens.
    Welcome, my lord. I dance attendance here.
57 I think the duke will not be spoke withal.
        Enter Catesby.
    Now, Catesby, what says your lord to my request?
CATESBY
    He doth entreat your grace, my noble lord,
60 To visit him tomorrow or next day.
    He is within, with two right reverend fathers,
62 Divinely bent to meditation,
    And in no worldly suits would he be moved
    To draw him from his holy exercise.
BUCKINGHAM
    Return, good Catesby, to the gracious duke;
    Tell him, myself, the mayor and aldermen,
    In deep designs, in matter of great moment,
68 No less importing than our general good,
    Are come to have some conference with his grace.
CATESBY
70 I'll signify so much unto him straight.   *Exit.*
BUCKINGHAM
    Ah ha, my lord, this prince is not an Edward.

---

49 *descant* improvised variation in music on a *ground* bass 51 *maid's* girl's;
answer . . . it i.e., keep saying no, but at the same time accept whatever is being
offered (misogynistic proverb, assuming that, although she says no, she does
want sexual intercourse) 55 *leads* sheets of metal used to cover a (flat) roof
57 *withal* with 62 *Divinely bent* (1) spiritually inclined, (2) kneeling like a
divine (cf. l. 73) 68 *No . . . than* i.e., of no less significance than

He is not lolling on a lewd love bed,
But on his knees at meditation;
Not dallying with a brace of courtesans,
But meditating with two deep divines;   75
Not sleeping, to engross his idle body,   76
But praying, to enrich his watchful soul.
Happy were England, would this virtuous prince
Take on his grace the sovereignty thereof.
But sure I fear we shall not win him to it.   80

MAYOR
Marry, God defend his grace should say us nay.   81

BUCKINGHAM
I fear he will. Here Catesby comes again.
    Enter Catesby.
Now, Catesby, what says his grace?

CATESBY   My lord,
He wonders to what end you have assembled
Such troops of citizens to come to him,
His grace not being warned thereof before.
He fears, my lord, you mean no good to him.

BUCKINGHAM
Sorry I am my noble cousin should
Suspect me that I mean no good to him.
By heaven, we come to him in perfect love;   90
And so once more return and tell his grace.
                                Exit [Catesby].
When holy and devout religious men
Are at their beads, 'tis much to draw them thence,   93
So sweet is zealous contemplation.
    Enter Richard aloft, between two Bishops.
    [Catesby returns.]

MAYOR
See where his grace stands, 'tween two clergymen.

---

75 *deep* i.e., spiritually and academically learned 76 *engross* fatten 81 *defend* forbid 93 *at their beads* saying their prayers; *'tis much* i.e., it takes a great deal

BUCKINGHAM
> Two props of virtue for a Christian prince,
97   To stay him from the fall of vanity;
> And see, a book of prayer in his hand –
99   True ornaments to know a holy man.
100   Famous Plantagenet, most gracious prince,
> Lend favorable ear to our requests,
> And pardon us the interruption
> Of thy devotion and right Christian zeal.

RICHARD
> My lord, there needs no such apology.
> I do beseech your grace to pardon me,
> Who, earnest in the service of my God,
> Deferred the visitation of my friends.
> But, leaving this, what is your grace's pleasure?

BUCKINGHAM
> Even that, I hope, which pleaseth God above
110   And all good men of this ungoverned isle.

RICHARD
> I do suspect I have done some offense
112   That seems disgracious in the city's eye,
> And that you come to reprehend my ignorance.

BUCKINGHAM
> You have, my lord. Would it might please your grace,
> On our entreaties, to amend your fault.

RICHARD
> Else wherefore breathe I in a Christian land?

BUCKINGHAM
> Know then it is your fault that you resign
> The supreme seat, the throne majestical,
> The sceptered office of your ancestors,
120   Your state of fortune and your due of birth,
> The lineal glory of your royal house,
> To the corruption of a blemished stock,

---

97 *fall of vanity* downfall caused by vanity 99 *ornaments* (referring to the clergymen and prayer book) 112 *disgracious* disliked 120 *state of fortune* position of greatness

Whiles, in the mildness of your sleepy thoughts,   123
Which here we waken to our country's good,
The noble isle doth want her proper limbs;   125
Her face defaced with scars of infamy,
Her royal stock graft with ignoble plants,
And almost shouldered in the swallowing gulf   128
Of dark forgetfulness and deep oblivion.
Which to recure, we heartily solicit   130
Your gracious self to take on you the charge
And kingly government of this your land,
Not as Protector, steward, substitute,
Or lowly factor for another's gain,   134
But as successively, from blood to blood,   135
Your right of birth, your empery, your own.   136
For this, consorted with the citizens,
Your very worshipful and loving friends,
And by their vehement instigation,
In this just cause come I to move your grace.   140

RICHARD
I cannot tell if to depart in silence,
Or bitterly to speak in your reproof,
Best fitteth my degree or your condition.   143
If not to answer, you might haply think
Tongue-tied ambition, not replying, yielded   145
To bear the golden yoke of sovereignty
Which fondly you would here impose on me.   147
If to reprove you for this suit of yours,
So seasoned with your faithful love to me,   149
Then, on the other side, I checked my friends.   150
Therefore – to speak, and to avoid the first,
And then, in speaking, not to incur the last –

---

123 *sleepy* contemplative 125 *proper* own 128 *shouldered in* violently jos-
tled into 130 *recure* restore to health 134 *factor* agent 135 *successively* in
order of succession 136 *empery* empire or sole rule 143 *fitteth . . . condition* accords with my rank (as duke) or your social position (as commoners)
145 *Tongue-tied . . . yielded* i.e., silence yields consent (proverbial) 147
fondly foolishly 149 *seasoned* made agreeable (given a pleasant taste) 150
checked rebuked

153   Definitively thus I answer you.
       Your love deserves my thanks, but my desert
       Unmeritable shuns your high request.
       First, if all obstacles were cut away,
157   And that my path were even to the crown,
       As the ripe revenue and due of birth,
159   Yet so much is my poverty of spirit,
160   So mighty and so many my defects,
       That I would rather hide me from my greatness,
162   Being a bark to brook no mighty sea,
163   Than in my greatness covet to be hid
       And in the vapor of my glory smothered.
       But, God be thanked, there is no need of me,
       And much I need to help you, were there need.
       The royal tree hath left us royal fruit,
       Which, mellowed by the stealing hours of time,
       Will well become the seat of majesty
170   And make, no doubt, us happy by his reign.
       On him I lay that you would lay on me,
172   The right and fortune of his happy stars,
       Which God defend that I should wring from him.

BUCKINGHAM
       My lord, this argues conscience in your grace,
175   But the respects thereof are nice and trivial,
       All circumstances well considerèd.
       You say that Edward is your brother's son;
       So say we too, but not by Edward's wife,
       For first was he contract to Lady Lucy –
180   Your mother lives a witness to his vow –
181   And afterward by substitute betrothed
       To Bona, sister to the King of France.

---

153 *Definitively* once and for all **157** *even* without impediment **159** *poverty of spirit* lack of self-assertion (perhaps meant also as an indirect compliment to himself, since "Blessed are the poor in spirit" [Matthew 5:3]) **162** *bark* small sailing vessel; *brook* endure **163** *Than . . . hid* than desire to be enveloped by my greatness **172** *happy* auspicious **175** *respects . . . nice* i.e., the considerations on which you argue are overscrupulous **181** *substitute* proxy

These both put off, a poor petitioner,
A care-crazed mother to a many sons,
A beauty-waning and distressèd widow,
Even in the afternoon of her best days,
Made prize and purchase of his wanton eye,   187
Seduced the pitch and height of his degree   188
To base declension and loathed bigamy.   189
By her in his unlawful bed he got   190
This Edward, whom our manners call the prince.
More bitterly could I expostulate,
Save that, for reverence to some alive,
I give a sparing limit to my tongue.
Then, good my lord, take to your royal self   195
This proffered benefit of dignity,
If not to bless us and the land withal,
Yet to draw forth your noble ancestry
From the corruption of abusing times
Unto a lineal true-derivèd course.   200

MAYOR
Do, good my lord; your citizens entreat you.

BUCKINGHAM
Refuse not, mighty lord, this proffered love.

CATESBY
O, make them joyful, grant their lawful suit!

RICHARD
Alas, why would you heap this care on me?
I am unfit for state and majesty.
I do beseech you take it not amiss,
I cannot nor I will not yield to you.

BUCKINGHAM
If you refuse it – as, in love and zeal,   208
Loath to depose the child, your brother's son,
As well we know your tenderness of heart   210

---

187 *purchase* booty 188 *Seduced . . . degree* i.e., led away (or down from)
the eminence and greatness associated with his noble rank 189 *declension*
falling away from a high standard 195 *good my lord* my good lord 208 *as*
i.e., as the result of being

211 And gentle, kind, effeminate remorse,
　　Which we have noted in you to your kindred
　　And equally indeed to all estates –
214 Yet know, whe'er you accept our suit or no,
　　Your brother's son shall never reign our king,
　　But we will plant some other in the throne
　　To the disgrace and downfall of your house;
　　And in this resolution here we leave you.
　　Come, citizens. Zounds, I'll entreat no more!

RICHARD
220 O, do not swear, my Lord of Buckingham.
　　　　　　　　Exeunt [Buckingham, Mayor, Aldermen,
　　　　　　　　　　　　　　　　　　and Citizens].

CATESBY
　　Call him again, sweet prince, accept their suit.
222 If you deny them, all the land will rue it.

RICHARD
　　Will you enforce me to a world of cares?
　　Call them again. *[Exit one or more.]* I am not made of
　　　stones,
　　But penetrable to your kind entreaties,
　　Albeit against my conscience and my soul.
　　　Enter Buckingham and the rest.
　　Cousin of Buckingham, and sage grave men,
　　Since you will buckle fortune on my back,
229 To bear her burden, whe'er I will or no,
230 I must have patience to endure the load.
　　But if black scandal or foul-faced reproach
232 Attend the sequel of your imposition,
233 Your mere enforcement shall acquittance me
　　From all the impure blots and stains thereof,
　　For God doth know, and you may partly see,

---

211 *kind, effeminate remorse* natural, tender pity (seen as feminine feelings)
214 *whe'er* whether 220 **s.d.** *Exeunt... Citizens* (they probably only start
to leave; ll. 221–26 are surely spoken for the Londoners to hear) 222 *rue*
suffer for 229 *To* i.e., to make me 232 *your imposition* i.e., the *fortune*
(kingship) you lay upon me 233 *mere* absolute; *acquittance* acquit

How far I am from the desire of this.

MAYOR
God bless your grace! We see it and will say it.

RICHARD
In saying so you shall but say the truth. ·

BUCKINGHAM
Then I salute you with this royal title –
Long live King Richard, England's worthy king!   240

ALL
Amen.

BUCKINGHAM
Tomorrow may it please you to be crowned?

RICHARD
Even when you please, for you will have it so.

BUCKINGHAM
Tomorrow then we will attend your grace,
And so most joyfully we take our leave.

RICHARD   *[To the Bishops]*
Come, let us to our holy work again. –
Farewell, my cousin; farewell, gentle friends.   *Exeunt.*

*

∾ **IV.1**   *Enter the Queen [Elizabeth], the Duchess of
York, and Marquess [of] Dorset [at one door]; Anne
Duchess of Gloucester [, Lady Margaret Plantagenet,
Clarence's young daughter, at another door].*

DUCHESS OF YORK
Who meets us here? My niece Plantagenet,   1
Led in the hand of her kind aunt of Gloucester?
Now, for my life, she's wand'ring to the Tower   3
On pure heart's love, to greet the tender prince.   4
Daughter, well met.   5

ANNE   God give your graces both

IV.1 Before the Tower 1 *niece* (in fact, granddaughter) 3 *for my life* i.e.,
staking my life upon it 4 *tender* young 5 *Daughter* daughter-in-law

A happy and a joyful time of day.

QUEEN ELIZABETH

7   As much to you, good sister. Whither away?

ANNE

No farther than the Tower, and, as I guess,
Upon the like devotion as yourselves,

10   To gratulate the gentle princes there.

QUEEN ELIZABETH

Kind sister, thanks. We'll enter all together.

Enter the Lieutenant [Brakenbury].

And in good time, here the lieutenant comes.
Master Lieutenant, pray you, by your leave,
How doth the prince and my young son of York?

BRAKENBURY

Right well, dear madam. By your patience,

16   I may not suffer you to visit them;
The king hath strictly charged the contrary.

QUEEN ELIZABETH

The king? Who's that?

BRAKENBURY   I mean the Lord Protector.

QUEEN ELIZABETH

19   The Lord protect him from that kingly title!

20   Hath he set bounds between their love and me?
I am their mother; who shall bar me from them?

DUCHESS OF YORK

I am their father's mother; I will see them.

ANNE

Their aunt I am in law, in love their mother;
Then bring me to their sights. I'll bear thy blame

25   And take thy office from thee on my peril.

BRAKENBURY

26   No, madam, no. I may not leave it so:
I am bound by oath, and therefore pardon me.

Exit [Brakenbury].

---

7 *sister* sister-in-law 10 *gratulate* greet 16 *suffer* permit 19 *The Lord . . . title* i.e., may God prevent Richard from getting the title of king 20 *bounds* barriers 25 *take . . . thee* i.e., take your office upon myself 26 *leave it* i.e., give up my office

Enter Stanley [Earl of Derby].

DERBY
Let me but meet you, ladies, one hour hence,
And I'll salute your grace of York as mother   29
And reverend looker-on of two fair queens.   30
    [To Anne]
Come, madam, you must straight to Westminster,   31
There to be crownèd Richard's royal queen.

QUEEN ELIZABETH
Ah, cut my lace asunder,   33
That my pent heart may have some scope to beat,
Or else I swoon with this dead-killing news.

ANNE
Despiteful tidings! O unpleasing news!

DORSET
Be of good cheer. Mother, how fares your grace?

QUEEN ELIZABETH
O Dorset, speak not to me, get thee gone.
Death and destruction dogs thee at thy heels;
Thy mother's name is ominous to children.   40
If thou wilt outstrip death, go cross the seas,
And live with Richmond, from the reach of hell.   42
Go, hie thee, hie thee from this slaughterhouse,
Lest thou increase the number of the dead
And make me die the thrall of Margaret's curse,   45
Nor mother, wife, nor England's counted queen.   46

DERBY
Full of wise care is this your counsel, madam.
    [To Dorset]
Take all the swift advantage of the hours.   48

---

29 *mother* mother-in-law **30** *looker-on* beholder; *two fair queens* Elizabeth,
wife of Edward IV, and Anne, wife of Richard III **31** *Westminster* Westminster Abbey, traditional place of coronation **33** *cut my lace* (Elizabethan
women wore tightly laced bodices) **40** *ominous* portending danger **42**
Richmond (Henry Tudor, Earl of Richmond, was living in exile in Brittany in
northern France) **45** *thrall* slave **46** *counted* esteemed **48** *Take . . . hours*
i.e., make full use of the time

49   You shall have letters from me to my son
50   In your behalf, to meet you on the way.
51   Be not ta'en tardy by unwise delay.

DUCHESS OF YORK
52   O ill-dispersing wind of misery!
53   O my accursèd womb, the bed of death!
54   A cockatrice hast thou hatched to the world,
       Whose unavoided eye is murderous.

DERBY
       Come, madam, come. I in all haste was sent.

ANNE
       And I with all unwillingness will go.
58   O, would to God that the inclusive verge
       Of golden metal that must round my brow
60   Were red-hot steel, to sear me to the brains.
61   Anointed let me be with deadly venom
       And die ere men can say, "God save the queen."

QUEEN ELIZABETH
       Go, go, poor soul. I envy not thy glory.
64   To feed my humor wish thyself no harm.

ANNE
       No? Why? When he that is my husband now
       Came to me as I followed Henry's corpse,
       When scarce the blood was well washed from his hands
       Which issued from my other angel husband
       And that dear saint which then I weeping followed –
70   O, when, I say, I looked on Richard's face,
       This was my wish: "Be thou," quoth I, "accursed
72   For making me, so young, so old a widow;
       And when thou wed'st, let sorrow haunt thy bed;
       And be thy wife, if any be so mad,

---

49 *son* stepson **51** *ta'en* taken, caught **52** *ill-dispersing* misfortune-scattering **53** *bed* birthplace **54** *cockatrice* basilisk (see I.2.150) **58** *inclusive verge* surrounding circle (i.e., the crown, with reference to the band of red-hot steel sometimes placed as punishment on the heads of traitors) **61** *Anointed* (anointing with holy oil was part of the ceremony of coronation) **64** *To . . . humor* to please me **72** *so young . . . widow* (being so young she will be a widow for a long time before she, too, dies)

More miserable by the life of thee
Than thou hast made me by my dear lord's death."
Lo, ere I can repeat this curse again,
Within so small a time, my woman's heart
Grossly grew captive to his honey words   79
And proved the subject of mine own soul's curse,   80
Which hitherto hath held mine eyes from rest,
For never yet one hour in his bed
Did I enjoy the golden dew of sleep,   83
But with his timorous dreams was still awaked.   84
Besides, he hates me for my father Warwick.
And will, no doubt, shortly be rid of me.

QUEEN ELIZABETH
Poor heart, adieu. I pity thy complaining.   87

ANNE
No more than with my soul I mourn for yours.

DORSET
Farewell, thou woeful welcomer of glory.

ANNE
Adieu, poor soul, that tak'st thy leave of it.   90

DUCHESS OF YORK *[To Dorset]*
Go thou to Richmond, and good fortune guide thee.
    [To Anne]
Go thou to Richard, and good angels tend thee.
    [To Queen Elizabeth]
Go thou to sanctuary, and good thoughts possess thee.
I to my grave, where peace and rest lie with me.
Eighty odd years of sorrow have I seen,
And each hour's joy wracked with a week of teen.   96

QUEEN ELIZABETH
Stay, yet look back with me unto the Tower.
Pity, you ancient stones, those tender babes
Whom envy hath immured within your walls –
Rough cradle for such little pretty ones,   100

---

79 *Grossly* stupidly 83 *golden dew* i.e., precious refreshment 84 *timorous*
full of fear; *still* continuously 87 *complaining* cause for complaint 96
wracked destroyed; *teen* grief

Rude ragged nurse, old sullen playfellow
For tender princes – use my babies well.
So foolish sorrows bids your stones farewell.   *Exeunt.*

*

~ **IV.2** *Sound a sennet. Enter Richard [as King], in*
pomp, [crowned,] Buckingham, Catesby, Ratcliffe,
Lovel [, a Page, and others].

KING RICHARD
1   Stand all apart. Cousin of Buckingham.
BUCKINGHAM
    My gracious sovereign?
KING RICHARD
    Give me thy hand.
        Sound [trumpets]. [Here he ascendeth the throne.]
                    Thus high, by thy advice
    And thy assistance is King Richard seated.
    But shall we wear these glories for a day?
    Or shall they last, and we rejoice in them?
BUCKINGHAM
    Still live they, and for ever let them last!
KING RICHARD
8   Ah, Buckingham, now do I play the touch,
    To try if thou be current gold indeed.
10   Young Edward lives. Think now what I would speak.
BUCKINGHAM
    Say on, my loving lord.
KING RICHARD
    Why, Buckingham, I say I would be king.
BUCKINGHAM
    Why, so you are, my thrice-renownèd liege.
KING RICHARD
    Ha! Am I king? 'Tis so. But Edward lives.

IV.2 The royal palace **s.d.** *sennet* a special set of notes on the trumpet used for
entrance and exit of processions **1** *apart* aside **8** *touch* touchstone (a
means of testing gold)

BUCKINGHAM

True, noble prince. 15

KING RICHARD O bitter consequence,

That Edward still should live "true noble prince."

Cousin, thou wast not wont to be so dull.

Shall I be plain? I wish the bastards dead,

And I would have it suddenly performed.

What sayst thou now? Speak suddenly, be brief. 20

BUCKINGHAM

Your grace may do your pleasure.

KING RICHARD

Tut, tut, thou art all ice; thy kindness freezes.

Say, have I thy consent that they shall die?

BUCKINGHAM

Give me some little breath, some pause, dear lord,

Before I positively speak in this.

I will resolve you herein presently. *Exit Buck[ingham].* 26

CATESBY *[Aside to another]*

The king is angry. See, he gnaws his lip.

KING RICHARD *[Aside]*

I will converse with iron-witted fools 28

And unrespective boys. None are for me

That look into me with considerate eyes. 30

High-reaching Buckingham grows circumspect.

Boy!

PAGE

My lord?

KING RICHARD

Know'st thou not any whom corrupting gold

Will tempt unto a close exploit of death?

PAGE

I know a discontented gentleman

Whose humble means match not his haughty spirit.

Gold were as good as twenty orators,

---

15 *consequence* conclusion 26 *presently* shortly 28–29 *iron-witted . . . un-respective* unfeeling . . . heedless 30 *considerate eyes* eyes that weigh my motives, seem thoughtful

And will, no doubt, tempt him to anything.

KING RICHARD

40 What is his name?

PAGE   His name, my lord, is Tyrrel.

KING RICHARD

I partly know the man. Go call him hither, boy.

Exit [Page].

[Aside]

42 The deep-revolving witty Buckingham
No more shall be the neighbor to my counsels.

44 Hath he so long held out with me, untired,
And stops he now for breath? Well, be it so.

Enter Stanley [Earl of Derby].

How now, Lord Stanley? What's the news?

DERBY   Know, my
loving lord,
The Marquess Dorset, as I hear, is fled
To Richmond in the parts where he abides.

[Stands aside.]

KING RICHARD

Come hither, Catesby. *[Aside to Catesby]* Rumor it abroad

50 That Anne my wife is very grievous sick.

51 I will take order for her keeping close.
Inquire me out some mean poor gentleman,
Whom I will marry straight to Clarence' daughter.

54 The boy is foolish, and I fear not him.
Look how thou dream'st! I say again, give out
That Anne, my queen, is sick and like to die.

57 About it, for it stands me much upon
To stop all hopes whose growth may damage me.

[Exit Catesby.]

[Aside]

59 I must be married to my brother's daughter,

---

42 *deep-revolving witty* deep-thinking, clever 44 *held out* i.e., lasted the course
51 *take . . . close* make arrangements for her imprisonment 54 *The boy* i.e.,
Clarence's son, Edward; *foolish* i.e., an idiot 57 *stands . . . upon* is of great importance to me 59 *brother's daughter* (Edward's daughter, Elizabeth, married
Richmond, later Henry VII, a match that united York and Lancaster)

Or else my kingdom stands on brittle glass: 60
Murder her brothers, and then marry her –
Uncertain way of gain! But I am in
So far in blood that sin will pluck on sin.
Tear-falling pity dwells not in this eye.   64
   Enter Tyrrel.
Is thy name Tyrrel?

TYRREL
James Tyrrel, and your most obedient subject.

KING RICHARD
  Art thou indeed?

TYRREL   Prove me, my gracious lord.

KING RICHARD
  Dar'st thou resolve to kill a friend of mine?

TYRREL
  Please you, but I had rather kill two enemies.   69

KING RICHARD
  Why, there thou hast it. Two deep enemies,   70
Foes to my rest and my sweet sleep's disturbers,
Are they that I would have thee deal upon;
Tyrrel, I mean those bastards in the Tower.

TYRREL
  Let me have open means to come to them,   74
And soon I'll rid you from the fear of them.

KING RICHARD
  Thou sing'st sweet music. Hark, come hither, Tyrrel.
Go, by this token. Rise, and lend thine ear.
   Whispers.
There is no more but so: say it is done,
And I will love thee and prefer thee for it.   79

TYRREL
  I will dispatch it straight.   *Exit.*   80
   Enter Buckingham.

BUCKINGHAM
  My lord, I have considered in my mind

---

64 *Tear-falling* i.e., weeping 69 *Please you* if it pleases you 74 *open* free 79
prefer promote

The late request that you did sound me in.

KING RICHARD

Well, let that rest. Dorset is fled to Richmond.

BUCKINGHAM

I hear the news, my lord.

KING RICHARD

85   Stanley, he is your wife's son. Well, look unto it.

BUCKINGHAM

My lord, I claim the gift, my due by promise,
For which your honor and your faith is pawned:
Th' earldom of Hereford and the movables
Which you have promisèd I shall possess.

KING RICHARD

90   Stanley, look to your wife. If she convey
Letters to Richmond, you shall answer it.

BUCKINGHAM

What says your highness to my just request?

KING RICHARD

93   I do remember me Henry the Sixth
Did prophesy that Richmond should be king
95   When Richmond was a little peevish boy.
A king! – perhaps – perhaps –

BUCKINGHAM

My lord –

KING RICHARD

How chance the prophet could not at that time
Have told me, I being by, that I should kill him?

BUCKINGHAM

100   My lord, your promise for the earldom.

KING RICHARD

Richmond! When last I was at Exeter,
The mayor in courtesy showed me the castle,
103   And called it Rouge-mount, at which name I started,

---

85 *he* i.e., Richmond   93–95 *I . . . boy* (see *Henry VI, Part 3*, IV.7.67–76)   95
peevish foolish   103 *Rouge-mount* i.e., Redhill (the incident is historical, but
the play on *Richmond* is forced)

Because a bard of Ireland told me once   104
I should not live long after I saw Richmond.

BUCKINGHAM
My lord –

KING RICHARD
Ay, what's o'clock?

BUCKINGHAM
I am thus bold to put your grace in mind
Of what you promised me.

KING RICHARD   Well, but what's o'clock?

BUCKINGHAM
Upon the stroke of ten.   110

KING RICHARD   Well, let it strike.

BUCKINGHAM
Why let it strike?

KING RICHARD
Because that like a jack thou keep'st the stroke   112
Betwixt thy begging and my meditation.
I am not in the giving vein today.

BUCKINGHAM
May it please you to resolve me in my suit.   115

KING RICHARD
Thou troublest me. I am not in the vein.

                                Exeunt [all but Buckingham].

BUCKINGHAM
And is it thus? Repays he my deep service
With such contempt? Made I him king for this?
O, let me think on Hastings, and be gone
To Brecknock while my fearful head is on.   *Exit.*   120

                                *

---

104 *bard* (the Celtic bards, or poets, were also considered prophets) 112
jack metal figure of a man that appeared to strike the hours on early clocks
(play on "lowbred fellow"; cf. *begging,* l. 113) 112–13 *keep'st . . . meditation*
(*like a jack* you) suspend the moment of striking (i.e., coming to the point in
your *begging* suit) and thus disturb my train of thought (so *let it strike,* l. 110)
115 *resolve* i.e., give a final answer 120 *Brecknock* the Buckingham family
seat at Brecon in Wales; *fearful* full of fears

∽ **IV.3** *Enter Tyrrel.*

TYRREL
 The tyrannous and bloody act is done,
2 The most arch deed of piteous massacre
 That ever yet this land was guilty of.
 Dighton and Forrest, who I did suborn
 To do this piece of ruthless butchery,
6 Albeit they were fleshed villains, bloody dogs,
 Melted with tenderness and mild compassion,
8 Wept like to children in their deaths' sad story.
 "O, thus," quoth Dighton, "lay the gentle babes."
10 "Thus, thus," quoth Forrest, "girdling one another
11 Within their alabaster innocent arms.
 Their lips were four red roses on a stalk,
 And in their summer beauty kissed each other.
 A book of prayers on their pillow lay,
 Which once," quoth Forrest, "almost changed my mind;
 But O, the devil" – there the villain stopped,
 When Dighton thus told on – "We smotherèd
18 The most replenishèd sweet work of nature
19 That from the prime creation e'er she framed."
20 Hence both are gone with conscience and remorse.
 They could not speak, and so I left them both,
 To bear this tidings to the bloody king.
  Enter [King] Richard.
 And here he comes. All health, my sovereign lord.
KING RICHARD
 Kind Tyrrel, am I happy in thy news?
TYRREL
 If to have done the thing you gave in charge
 Beget your happiness, be happy then,
 For it is done.

IV.3 (No clear textual indication of the setting.) **2** *most arch* chiefest **6** *fleshed* experienced (like hunting *dogs*) **8** *their deaths' sad story* the sad account of their deaths **11** *alabaster* white **18** *replenishèd* complete (in the sense of being full of virtues and beauty) **19** *prime* first

KING RICHARD But didst thou see them dead?

TYRREL
  I did, my lord.

KING RICHARD And buried, gentle Tyrrel?

TYRREL
  The chaplain of the Tower hath buried them;
  But where, to say the truth, I do not know.   30

KING RICHARD
  Come to me, Tyrrel, soon at after-supper,   31
  When thou shalt tell the process of their death.   32
  Meantime, but think how I may do thee good,
  And be inheritor of thy desire.   34
  Farewell till then.

TYRREL   I humbly take my leave.   *[Exit.]*

KING RICHARD
  The son of Clarence have I pent up close,
  His daughter meanly have I matched in marriage,
  The sons of Edward sleep in Abraham's bosom,
  And Anne my wife hath bid this world good night.
  Now, for I know the Breton Richmond aims   40
  At young Elizabeth, my brother's daughter,
  And by that knot looks proudly on the crown,   42
  To her go I, a jolly thriving wooer.
    Enter Ratcliffe.

RATCLIFFE
  My lord –

KING RICHARD
  Good or bad news, that thou com'st in so bluntly?

RATCLIFFE
  Bad news, my lord. Morton is fled to Richmond,   46
  And Buckingham, backed with the hardy Welshmen,
  Is in the field, and still his power increaseth.

KING RICHARD
  Ely with Richmond troubles me more near

---

31 *after-supper* dessert 32 *process* story 34 *be* you shall be 40 *for* because
42 *knot* i.e., marriage 46 *Morton* Bishop of Ely

50 Than Buckingham and his rash-levied strength.
51 Come, I have learned that fearful commenting
    Is leaden servitor to dull delay.
53 Delay leads impotent and snail-paced beggary.
54 Then fiery expedition be my wing,
55 Jove's Mercury, and herald for a king.
56 Go, muster men. My counsel is my shield.
    We must be brief when traitors brave the field. *Exeunt.*

                              *

❧ **IV.4** *Enter old Queen Margaret.*

QUEEN MARGARET
1   So now prosperity begins to mellow
    And drop into the rotten mouth of death.
    Here in these confines slyly have I lurked
    To watch the waning of mine enemies.
5   A dire induction am I witness to,
6   And will to France, hoping the consequence
7   Will prove as bitter, black, and tragical.
    Withdraw thee, wretched Margaret. Who comes here?
    [Retires.]
    Enter Duchess [of York] and Queen [Elizabeth].

QUEEN ELIZABETH
    Ah, my poor princes! ah, my tender babes!
10 My unblown flowers, new-appearing sweets!
    If yet your gentle souls fly in the air
12 And be not fixed in doom perpetual,
    Hover about me with your airy wings

---

50 *rash-levied strength* hastily raised army 51–52 *fearful . . . servitor* timorous talk is the sluggish attendant 53 *beggary* ruin 54 *expedition* speed 55 *Mercury* messenger of the gods (note Richard's neat equation of himself with *Jove*, king of the gods) 56 *counsel* adviser
IV.4 Before the royal palace 1–2 *So . . . death* (image taken from ripe fruit falling and rotting on the ground) 5 *induction* (1) beginning (as of a play), (2) plan 6 *consequence* conclusion (as the catastrophe of a play) 7 *as* equally 10 *unblown* unopened; *sweets* fragrant flowers 12 *fixed . . . perpetual* i.e., assigned by God's judgment to their final place of punishment or reward

And hear your mother's lamentation.

QUEEN MARGARET   *[Aside]*
Hover about her. Say that right for right
Hath dimmed your infant morn to agèd night.

DUCHESS OF YORK
So many miseries have crazed my voice   17
That my woe-wearied tongue is still and mute.
Edward Plantagenet, why art thou dead?

QUEEN MARGARET   *[Aside]*
Plantagenet doth quit Plantagenet;   20
Edward for Edward pays a dying debt.   21

QUEEN ELIZABETH
Wilt thou, O God, fly from such gentle lambs
And throw them in the entrails of the wolf?
When didst thou sleep when such a deed was done?   24

QUEEN MARGARET   *[Aside]*
When holy Harry died, and my sweet son.   25

DUCHESS OF YORK
Dead life, blind sight, poor mortal-living ghost,   26
Woe's scene, world's shame, grave's due by life usurped,   27
Brief abstract and record of tedious days,   28
Rest thy unrest on England's lawful earth,
Unlawfully made drunk with innocent blood.   30
    [Sits down.]

QUEEN ELIZABETH
Ah that thou wouldst as soon afford a grave
As thou canst yield a melancholy seat.
Then would I hide my bones, not rest them here.
Ah, who hath any cause to mourn but we?
    [Sits down by her.]

QUEEN MARGARET   *[Comes forward.]*
If ancient sorrow be most reverend,

---

17 *crazed* cracked 20 *quit* make up for 21 *Edward for Edward* Elizabeth's
son, Prince Edward, for Margaret's son, Edward, Prince of Wales; *dying
debt* i.e., a debt for which the payment is death 24 *When* when ever (before this
time) 25 *Harry* (her husband, King Henry VI) 26 *mortal-living* dead-alive
27 *grave's . . . usurped* i.e., someone who should be dead still alive 28 *Brief
abstract* summary (*Brief* may also be intended to limit *record*)

36 Give mine the benefit of seniory
37 And let my griefs frown on the upper hand.
    If sorrow can admit society,
39 Tell over your woes again by viewing mine.
40 I had an Edward, till a Richard killed him;
41 I had a husband, till a Richard killed him:
        [To Queen Elizabeth]
42 Thou hadst an Edward, till a Richard killed him;
43 Thou hadst a Richard, till a Richard killed him.

DUCHESS OF YORK
44 I had a Richard too, and thou didst kill him;
45 I had a Rutland too, thou holp'st to kill him.

QUEEN MARGARET
    Thou hadst a Clarence too, and Richard killed him.
    From forth the kennel of thy womb hath crept
    A hellhound that doth hunt us all to death:
    That dog, that had his teeth before his eyes,
50 To worry lambs and lap their gentle blood,
    That foul defacer of God's handiwork,
52 That excellent grand tyrant of the earth
53 That reigns in gallèd eyes of weeping souls,
    Thy womb let loose to chase us to our graves.
    O upright, just, and true-disposing God,
56 How do I thank thee that this charnel cur
    Preys on the issue of his mother's body
58 And makes her pew fellow with others' moan.

DUCHESS OF YORK
    O Harry's wife, triumph not in my woes.
60 God witness with me, I have wept for thine.

---

36 *seniory* seniority **37** *frown . . . hand* i.e., have the mastery in looking grim or dismal **39** *Tell over* count **40** *Edward* Prince of Wales; *Richard* Duke of Gloucester **41** *husband* King Henry VI **42** *Edward* Prince Edward **43** *Richard* Duke of York (killed by Richard, Duke of Gloucester) **44** *Richard* (a different Duke of York, her husband) **45** *Rutland* (her youngest son; his death and that of his father are shown in *3 Henry VI*, I.3 and I.4); *holp'st* helped **52** *excellent* preeminently **53** *reigns . . . souls* i.e., flourishes (as a ruler) upon the tears wept from sore eyes of those individuals (whom he has injured) **56** *charnel* (of the charnel house, tomb) **58** *pew fellow* companion

QUEEN MARGARET
  Bear with me. I am hungry for revenge,
  And now I cloy me with beholding it.
  Thy Edward he is dead, that killed my Edward;
  Thy other Edward dead, to quit my Edward;   64
  Young York he is but boot, because both they   65
  Matched not the high perfection of my loss.
  Thy Clarence he is dead that stabbed my Edward,
  And the beholders of this frantic play,
  Th' adulterate Hastings, Rivers, Vaughan, Grey,   69
  Untimely smothered in their dusky graves.   70
  Richard yet lives, hell's black intelligencer,   71
  Only reserved their factor to buy souls   72
  And send them thither. But at hand, at hand,
  Ensues his piteous and unpitied end.
  Earth gapes, hell burns, fiends roar, saints pray,   75
  To have him suddenly conveyed from hence.
  Cancel his bond of life, dear God, I pray,
  That I may live and say, "The dog is dead."

QUEEN ELIZABETH
  O, thou didst prophesy the time would come
  That I should wish for thee to help me curse   80
  That bottled spider, that foul bunch-backed toad.

QUEEN MARGARET
  I called thee then vain flourish of my fortune;
  I called thee then poor shadow, painted queen,
  The presentation of but what I was,
  The flattering index of a direful pageant,   85
  One heaved a-high to be hurled down below,
  A mother only mocked with two fair babes,
  A dream of what thou wast, a garish flag,   88

---

64 *quit* requite 65 *but boot* i.e., thrown in as an extra 69 *adulterate* guilty
of adultery 71 *intelligencer* secret agent 72 *Only . . . factor* only retained as
their agent 75–77 *Earth . . . pray* (Shakespeare seems to be thinking of the
conclusion of Marlowe's *Doctor Faustus*) 85 *index* prologue; *pageant* play or
show 88–89 *garish . . . shot* brightly colored standard-bearer (an appearance only, thus picking up *painted queen*, l. 83) who draws the fire of all enemies

To be the aim of every dangerous shot,
90 A sign of dignity, a breath, a bubble,
91 A queen in jest, only to fill the scene.
Where is thy husband now? Where be thy brothers?
Where be thy two sons? Wherein dost thou joy?
Who sues and kneels and says, "God save the queen"?
95 Where be the bending peers that flattered thee?
Where be the thronging troops that followed thee?
97 Decline all this, and see what now thou art:
For happy wife, a most distressèd widow;
For joyful mother, one that wails the name;
100 For one being sued to, one that humbly sues;
101 For queen, a very caitiff crowned with care;
For she that scorned at me, now scorned of me;
For she being feared of all, now fearing one;
For she commanding all, obeyed of none.
Thus hath the course of justice whirled about
And left thee but a very prey to time,
Having no more but thought of what thou wast,
To torture thee the more, being what thou art.
Thou didst usurp my place, and dost thou not
110 Usurp the just proportion of my sorrow?
111 Now thy proud neck bears half my burdened yoke,
From which even here I slip my weary head
And leave the burden of it all on thee.
Farewell, York's wife, and queen of sad mischance.
These English woes shall make me smile in France.

QUEEN ELIZABETH
O thou well skilled in curses, stay awhile
And teach me how to curse mine enemies.

QUEEN MARGARET
Forbear to sleep the nights, and fast the days;
Compare dead happiness with living woe;
120 Think that thy babes were sweeter than they were
And he that slew them fouler than he is.

---

91 *queen . . . scene* i.e., a mute player-queen 95 *bending* bowing 97 *Decline* run through in order 101 *caitiff* wretch 111 *burdened* burdensome

Bett'ring thy loss makes the bad causer worse.   122
Revolving this will teach thee how to curse.

QUEEN ELIZABETH
My words are dull. O, quicken them with thine!   124

QUEEN MARGARET
Thy woes will make them sharp and pierce like mine.
                                    Exit [Queen] Margaret.

DUCHESS OF YORK
Why should calamity be full of words?

QUEEN ELIZABETH
Windy attorneys to their clients' woes,   127
Airy succeeders of intestate joys,   128
Poor breathing orators of miseries,
Let them have scope. Though what they will impart   130
Help nothing else, yet do they ease the heart.

DUCHESS OF YORK
If so, then be not tongue-tied; go with me,
And in the breath of bitter words let's smother
My damnèd son that thy two sweet sons smothered.
      [A march within.]
The trumpet sounds. Be copious in exclaims.
      *Enter King Richard and his train [marching, with
      Drums and Trumpets].*

KING RICHARD
Who intercepts me in my expedition?   136

DUCHESS OF YORK
O, she that might have intercepted thee,
By strangling thee in her accursèd womb,
From all the slaughters, wretch, that thou hast done.

QUEEN ELIZABETH
Hid'st thou that forehead with a golden crown   140
Where should be branded, if that right were right,
The slaughter of the prince that owed that crown   142

---

122 *Bett'ring . . . worse* i.e., magnifying thy loss makes the perpetrator of the
evil appear even worse than he is 124 *quicken* put life into 127 *Windy . . .
woes* (words are) airy pleaders for the woes of their clients 128 *succeeders . . .
joys* heirs of joys that died without bequeathing anything in a will 136 *expedition* (1) military undertaking, (2) haste 142 *owed* possessed by right

And the dire death of my poor sons and brothers?
144 Tell me, thou villain-slave, where are my children?
DUCHESS OF YORK
Thou toad, thou toad, where is thy brother Clarence?
And little Ned Plantagenet, his son?
QUEEN ELIZABETH
Where is the gentle Rivers, Vaughan, Grey?
DUCHESS OF YORK
Where is kind Hastings?
KING RICHARD
149 A flourish, trumpets! Strike alarum, drums!
150 Let not the heavens hear these telltale women
Rail on the Lord's anointed. Strike, I say!
Flourish. Alarums.
Either be patient and entreat me fair,
153 Or with the clamorous report of war
Thus will I drown your exclamations.
DUCHESS OF YORK
Art thou my son?
KING RICHARD
Ay, I thank God, my father, and yourself.
DUCHESS OF YORK
Then patiently hear my impatience.
KING RICHARD
158 Madam, I have a touch of your condition
159 That cannot brook the accent of reproof.
DUCHESS OF YORK
160 O, let me speak.
KING RICHARD   Do then, but I'll not hear.
DUCHESS OF YORK
I will be mild and gentle in my words.
KING RICHARD
And brief, good mother, for I am in haste.

---

144 *villain-slave* lowest criminal (with suggestions of "lowbred" in *villain* [serf] and *slave*) 149 *alarum* call to arms 153 *report* noise 158 *condition* temperament 159 *brook* endure; *accent* language

DUCHESS OF YORK
Art thou so hasty? I have stayed for thee,   163
God knows, in torment and in agony.

KING RICHARD
And came I not at last to comfort you?

DUCHESS OF YORK
No, by the Holy Rood, thou know'st it well,   166
Thou cam'st on earth to make the earth my hell.
A grievous burden was thy birth to me;
Tetchy and wayward was thy infancy;   169
Thy schooldays frightful, desp'rate, wild, and furious;   170
Thy prime of manhood daring, bold, and venturous;
Thy age confirmed, proud, subtle, sly, and bloody,   172
More mild, but yet more harmful, kind in hatred.
What comfortable hour canst thou name
That ever graced me with thy company?

KING RICHARD
Faith, none, but Humphrey Hour, that called your grace   176
To breakfast once, forth of my company.   177
If I be so disgracious in your eye,   178
Let me march on and not offend you, madam.
Strike up the drum.   180

DUCHESS OF YORK   I prithee hear me speak.

KING RICHARD
You speak too bitterly.

DUCHESS OF YORK   Hear me a word,
For I shall never speak to thee again.

KING RICHARD
So.

DUCHESS OF YORK
Either thou wilt die by God's just ordinance

---

163 *stayed* waited 166 *Holy Rood* Christ's cross 169 *Tetchy and wayward*
fretful and willful 170 *frightful* full of fears 172 *age confirmed* i.e., having
reached full maturity 176 *Humphrey Hour* (meaning uncertain; perhaps
"that hour when you were paradoxically without food" [cf. "dining with
Duke Humphrey": going hungry] or, more likely, a now irrecoverable joke
on an individual's name) 177 *forth* out 178 *disgracious* unpleasing

Ere from this war thou turn a conqueror,
Or I with grief and extreme age shall perish
And never more behold thy face again.
Therefore take with thee my most grievous curse,
Which in the day of battle tire thee more
190 Than all the complete armor that thou wear'st.
My prayers on the adverse party fight,
And there the little souls of Edward's children
Whisper the spirits of thine enemies
And promise them success and victory.
Bloody thou art, bloody will be thy end;
Shame serves thy life and doth thy death attend.   *Exit.*

QUEEN ELIZABETH
Though far more cause, yet much less spirit to curse
Abides in me. I say amen to her.

KING RICHARD
Stay, madam. I must talk a word with you.

QUEEN ELIZABETH
200 I have no more sons of the royal blood
For thee to slaughter. For my daughters, Richard,
They shall be praying nuns, not weeping queens,
203 And therefore level not to hit their lives.

KING RICHARD
You have a daughter called Elizabeth,
Virtuous and fair, royal and gracious.

QUEEN ELIZABETH
And must she die for this? O, let her live,
207 And I'll corrupt her manners, stain her beauty,
Slander myself as false to Edward's bed,
Throw over her the veil of infamy;
210 So she may live unscarred of bleeding slaughter,
I will confess she was not Edward's daughter.

KING RICHARD
Wrong not her birth; she is a royal princess.

---

190 *complete armor* i.e., a full suit of armor, from head to foot 203 *level . . .
lives* i.e., do not take aim to kill them 207 *manners* moral character

QUEEN ELIZABETH
To save her life, I'll say she is not so.

KING RICHARD
Her life is safest only in her birth.   214

QUEEN ELIZABETH
And only in that safety died her brothers.

KING RICHARD
Lo, at their birth good stars were opposite.

QUEEN ELIZABETH
No, to their lives ill friends were contrary.   217

KING RICHARD
All unavoided is the doom of destiny.   218

QUEEN ELIZABETH
True, when avoided grace makes destiny.   219
My babes were destined to a fairer death   220
If grace had blessed thee with a fairer life.

KING RICHARD
You speak as if that I had slain my cousins.

QUEEN ELIZABETH
Cousins indeed, and by their uncle cozened   223
Of comfort, kingdom, kindred, freedom, life.
Whose hand soever lanced their tender hearts,   225
Thy head, all indirectly, gave direction.   226
No doubt the murd'rous knife was dull and blunt
Till it was whetted on thy stone-hard heart
To revel in the entrails of my lambs.
But that still use of grief makes wild grief tame,   230
My tongue should to thy ears not name my boys
Till that my nails were anchored in thine eyes;
And I, in such a desp'rate bay of death,   233
Like a poor bark of sails and tackling reft,   234

---

214 *only in* only because of 217 *contrary* opposed 218 *unavoided* un-
avoidable; *doom* lot 219 *avoided grace* one who has rejected God's grace
(i.e., Richard) 223 *cozened* cheated or betrayed 225 *lanced* pierced 226
all indirectly i.e., even if not in express terms 230 *But that still* except that
continual 233 *bay* inlet (with play on the hunting term "at bay": driven to
a last stand) 234 *bark* boat; *reft* deprived

Rush all to pieces on thy rocky bosom.

KING RICHARD

Madam, so thrive I in my enterprise
And dangerous success of bloody wars
As I intend more good to you and yours
Than ever you or yours by me were harmed.

QUEEN ELIZABETH

240 What good is covered with the face of heaven,
To be discovered, that can do me good?

KING RICHARD

Th' advancement of your children, gentle lady.

QUEEN ELIZABETH

Up to some scaffold, there to lose their heads.

KING RICHARD

Unto the dignity and height of fortune,
245 The high imperial type of this earth's glory.

QUEEN ELIZABETH

Flatter my sorrow with report of it.
Tell me, what state, what dignity, what honor
248 Canst thou demise to any child of mine?

KING RICHARD

Even all I have – ay, and myself and all –
250 Will I withal endow a child of thine,
251 So in the Lethe of thy angry soul
Thou drown the sad remembrance of those wrongs
Which thou supposest I have done to thee.

QUEEN ELIZABETH

254 Be brief, lest that the process of thy kindness
255 Last longer telling than thy kindness' date.

KING RICHARD

256 Then know that from my soul I love thy daughter.

---

240 *What . . . heaven* i.e., what good is yet to be found in this world (not already discovered) 245 *type* symbol 248 *demise* transmit 251 *Lethe* river in hell (to drink of which induced forgetfulness) 254 *process* story 255 *telling* in telling; *date* duration 256 *from my soul* with my very soul (but Queen Elizabeth takes Richard to mean that his love is "from" [i.e., separated from] his inmost feelings)

QUEEN ELIZABETH
My daughter's mother thinks it with her soul.
KING RICHARD
What do you think?
QUEEN ELIZABETH
That thou dost love my daughter from thy soul.
So from thy soul's love didst thou love her brothers,   260
And from my heart's love I do thank thee for it.
KING RICHARD
Be not so hasty to confound my meaning.   262
I mean that with my soul I love thy daughter
And do intend to make her Queen of England.
QUEEN ELIZABETH
Well then, who dost thou mean shall be her king?
KING RICHARD
Even he that makes her queen. Who else should be?
QUEEN ELIZABETH
What, thou?
KING RICHARD   Even so. How think you of it?
QUEEN ELIZABETH
How canst thou woo her?
KING RICHARD   That would I learn of you,
As one being best acquainted with her humor.   269
QUEEN ELIZABETH
And wilt thou learn of me?   270
KING RICHARD   Madam, with all my heart.
QUEEN ELIZABETH
Send to her by the man that slew her brothers
A pair of bleeding hearts; thereon engrave
"Edward" and "York"; then haply will she weep.
Therefore present to her – as sometimes Margaret
Did to thy father, steeped in Rutland's blood –
A handkerchief, which say to her did drain
The purple sap from her sweet brother's body,   277

---

262 *confound* misconstrue   269 *humor* temperament   277 *sap* blood

278 And bid her wipe her weeping eyes withal.
If this inducement move her not to love,
280 Send her a letter of thy noble deeds.
Tell her thou mad'st away her uncle Clarence,
Her uncle Rivers, ay, and for her sake,
283 Mad'st quick conveyance with her good aunt Anne.

KING RICHARD
You mock me, madam. This is not the way
To win your daughter.

QUEEN ELIZABETH   There is no other way,
Unless thou couldst put on some other shape,
And not be Richard that hath done all this.

KING RICHARD
Say that I did all this for love of her.

QUEEN ELIZABETH
Nay, then indeed she cannot choose but hate thee,
290 Having bought love with such a bloody spoil.

KING RICHARD
291 Look what is done cannot be now amended.
Men shall deal unadvisedly sometimes,
Which after-hours gives leisure to repent.
If I did take the kingdom from your sons,
To make amends I'll give it to your daughter.
If I have killed the issue of your womb,
297 To quicken your increase I will beget
Mine issue of your blood upon your daughter.
A grandam's name is little less in love
300 Than is the doting title of a mother.
They are as children but one step below,
302 Even of your metal, of your very blood,
Of all one pain, save for a night of groans
304 Endured of her for whom you bid like sorrow.
Your children were vexation to your youth,

---

278 *withal* with (it) 283 *quick conveyance with* speedy removal of 290
spoil slaughter (hunting term: the breaking up of the quarry after the kill)
291 *Look what* whatever 297 *quicken your increase* i.e., give new life to your
(dead) offspring 302 *metal* substance 304 *of* by; *bid* underwent, suffered

But mine shall be a comfort to your age.
The loss you have is but a son being king,
And by that loss your daughter is made queen.
I cannot make you what amends I would;
Therefore accept such kindness as I can.   310
Dorset your son, that with a fearful soul   311
Leads discontented steps in foreign soil,
This fair alliance quickly shall call home
To high promotions and great dignity.
The king, that calls your beauteous daughter wife,
Familiarly shall call thy Dorset brother.
Again shall you be mother to a king,
And all the ruins of distressful times
Repaired with double riches of content.
What! We have many goodly days to see.   320
The liquid drops of tears that you have shed
Shall come again, transformed to orient pearl,   322
Advantaging their loan with interest   323
Of ten times double gain of happiness.
Go then, my mother, to thy daughter go.
Make bold her bashful years with your experience;
Prepare her ears to hear a wooer's tale;
Put in her tender heart th' aspiring flame
Of golden sovereignty; acquaint the princess
With the sweet silent hours of marriage joys,   330
And when this arm of mine hath chastisèd
The petty rebel, dull-brained Buckingham,
Bound with triumphant garlands will I come   333
And lead thy daughter to a conqueror's bed –
To whom I will retail my conquest won,   335
And she shall be sole victoress, Caesar's Caesar.

QUEEN ELIZABETH
    What were I best to say? Her father's brother

---

310 *can* i.e., am able to give 311 *fearful* full of fears 322 *orient* shining
323 *Advantaging* increasing 333 *triumphant garlands* i.e., garlands befitting
a military triumph (in the Roman sense) 335 *retail* recount (though Shakespeare would seem to mean "transmit")

Would be her lord? Or shall I say her uncle?
Or he that slew her brothers and her uncles?
340 Under what title shall I woo for thee
That God, the law, my honor, and her love
Can make seem pleasing to her tender years?

KING RICHARD
343 Infer fair England's peace by this alliance.

QUEEN ELIZABETH
Which she shall purchase with still-lasting war.

KING RICHARD
Tell her the king, that may command, entreats.

QUEEN ELIZABETH
That at her hands which the king's King forbids.

KING RICHARD
Say she shall be a high and mighty queen.

QUEEN ELIZABETH
348 To vail the title, as her mother doth.

KING RICHARD
Say I will love her everlastingly.

QUEEN ELIZABETH
350 But how long shall that title "ever" last?

KING RICHARD
Sweetly in force unto her fair life's end.

QUEEN ELIZABETH
But how long fairly shall her sweet life last?

KING RICHARD
As long as heaven and nature lengthens it.

QUEEN ELIZABETH
As long as hell and Richard likes of it.

KING RICHARD
Say I, her sovereign, am her subject low.

QUEEN ELIZABETH
356 But she, your subject, loathes such sovereignty.

KING RICHARD
Be eloquent in my behalf to her.

---

343 *Infer* imply 348 *vail* submit 356 *sovereignty* (1) rule, (2) ruler (i.e., Richard)

QUEEN ELIZABETH
  An honest tale speeds best being plainly told.
KING RICHARD
  Then plainly to her tell my loving tale.
QUEEN ELIZABETH
  Plain and not honest is too harsh a style.   360
KING RICHARD
  Your reasons are too shallow and too quick.
QUEEN ELIZABETH
  O no, my reasons are too deep and dead –
  Too deep and dead, poor infants, in their graves.
KING RICHARD
  Harp not on that string, madam; that is past.
QUEEN ELIZABETH
  Harp on it still shall I till heartstrings break.
KING RICHARD
  Now, by my George, my garter, and my crown –   366
QUEEN ELIZABETH
  Profaned, dishonored, and the third usurped.
KING RICHARD
  I swear –
QUEEN ELIZABETH   By nothing, for this is no oath:
  Thy George, profaned, hath lost his holy honor;
  Thy garter, blemished, pawned his knightly virtue;   370
  Thy crown, usurped, disgraced his kingly glory.
  If something thou wouldst swear to be believed,
  Swear then by something that thou hast not wronged.
KING RICHARD
  Then by myself –
QUEEN ELIZABETH   Thyself is self-misused.
KING RICHARD
  Now by the world –
QUEEN ELIZABETH   'Tis full of thy foul wrongs.

---

360 *Plain . . . style* i.e., (1) plain style (cf. the proverb "Truth is plain") unless
it is sincere will be too harsh, (2) lies (i.e., things not honest) need the deco-
rated style   366 *George . . . garter* (a jeweled pendant with the figure of Saint
George and the gold collar from which it hung were parts of the insignia of
the Order of the Garter, the highest order of knighthood)

KING RICHARD
  My father's death –
QUEEN ELIZABETH   Thy life hath it dishonored.
KING RICHARD
  Why then, by God –
QUEEN ELIZABETH   God's wrong is most of all.
  If thou didst fear to break an oath with him,
379 The unity the king my husband made
380 Thou hadst not broken, nor my brothers died.
  If thou hadst feared to break an oath by him,
382 Th' imperial metal, circling now thy head,
  Had graced the tender temples of my child,
  And both the princes had been breathing here,
  Which now, two tender bedfellows for dust,
  Thy broken faith hath made the prey for worms.
  What canst thou swear by now?
KING RICHARD   The time to come.
QUEEN ELIZABETH
  That thou hast wrongèd in the time o'erpast,
  For I myself have many tears to wash
390 Hereafter time, for time past wronged by thee.
  The children live whose fathers thou hast slaughtered,
392 Ungoverned youth, to wail it in their age;
  The parents live whose children thou hast butchered,
  Old barren plants, to wail it with their age.
  Swear not by time to come, for that thou hast
  Misused ere used, by times ill-used o'erpast.
KING RICHARD
397 As I intend to prosper and repent,
  So thrive I in my dangerous affairs
  Of hostile arms. Myself myself confound,
400 Heaven and fortune bar me happy hours.
  Day, yield me not thy light, nor, night, thy rest.

---

379 *unity* (the "reconciliation" in II.1) 382 *imperial metal* i.e., royal crown
390 *Hereafter* future 392 *Ungoverned* i.e., without parents to guide them
397–98 *As . . . So* to the degree I mean to do well and repent, to such a degree 397–405 *As . . . daughter* (note that Richard here in effect curses himself, bringing the curses in this scene to a final focus)

Be opposite all planets of good luck
To my proceeding if, with dear heart's love,
Immaculate devotion, holy thoughts,
I tender not thy beauteous princely daughter.
In her consists my happiness and thine.
Without her, follows to myself and thee,
Herself, the land, and many a Christian soul,
Death, desolation, ruin, and decay.
It cannot be avoided but by this;   410
It will not be avoided but by this.
Therefore, dear mother – I must call you so –
Be the attorney of my love to her:
Plead what I will be, not what I have been –
Not my deserts, but what I will deserve;
Urge the necessity and state of times,
And be not peevish-fond in great designs.   417

QUEEN ELIZABETH
Shall I be tempted of the devil thus?

KING RICHARD
Ay, if the devil tempt you to do good.

QUEEN ELIZABETH
Shall I forget myself to be myself?   420

KING RICHARD
Ay, if yourself's remembrance wrong yourself.

QUEEN ELIZABETH
Yet thou didst kill my children.

KING RICHARD
But in your daughter's womb I bury them,
Where, in that nest of spicery, they will breed   424
Selves of themselves, to your recomforture.   425

QUEEN ELIZABETH
Shall I go win my daughter to thy will?

KING RICHARD
And be a happy mother by the deed.

---

417 *peevish-fond* foolishly self-willed   420 *Shall . . . be myself* i.e., shall I forget who I am   424 *spicery* fragrant spices   424–25 *they . . . themselves* (like the phoenix, which bred from itself)   425 *recomforture* consolation

QUEEN ELIZABETH
I go. Write to me very shortly,
And you shall understand from me her mind.

KING RICHARD
430   Bear her my true love's kiss *[He kisses her.]* – and so
farewell.   *Exit Q[ueen Elizabeth].*
431   Relenting fool, and shallow, changing woman!
Enter Ratcliffe [,Catesby following].
How now? What news?

RATCLIFFE
Most mighty sovereign, on the western coast
434   Rideth a puissant navy. To our shores
Throng many doubtful hollow-hearted friends,
436   Unarmed, and unresolved to beat them back.
437   'Tis thought that Richmond is their admiral;
438   And there they hull, expecting but the aid
Of Buckingham to welcome them ashore.

KING RICHARD
440   Some light-foot friend post to the Duke of Norfolk.
441   Ratcliffe, thyself – or Catesby – where is he?

CATESBY
Here, my good lord.

KING RICHARD   Catesby, fly to the duke.

CATESBY
I will, my lord, with all convenient haste.

KING RICHARD
Ratcliffe, come hither. Post to Salisbury.
When thou com'st thither –
[To Catesby]   Dull unmindful villain,
Why stay'st thou here and go'st not to the duke?

CATESBY
First, mighty liege, tell me your highness' pleasure,

---

431 *shallow* superficial 434 *puissant* mighty 436 *unresolved* undetermined
how to act 437 *their admiral* i.e., of the *navy* of l. 434 438 *hull* drift with
the winds 441 *Ratcliffe . . . he* (Catesby may have entered with Ratcliffe at
l. 43 or, possibly, entered with King Richard as part of his *train*)

What from your grace I shall deliver to him.
KING RICHARD
  O, true, good Catesby. Bid him levy straight
  The greatest strength and power that he can make   450
  And meet me suddenly at Salisbury.
CATESBY
  I go.   *Exit.*
RATCLIFFE
  What, may it please you, shall I do at Salisbury?
KING RICHARD
  Why, what wouldst thou do there before I go?
RATCLIFFE
  Your highness told me I should post before.   455
KING RICHARD
  My mind is changed.
    Enter Lord Stanley [Earl of Derby].
                      Stanley, what news with you?
DERBY
  None, good my liege, to please you with the hearing,
  Nor none so bad but well may be reported.
KING RICHARD
  Hoyday, a riddle! Neither good nor bad!
  What need'st thou run so many miles about,   460
  When thou mayest tell thy tale the nearest way?
  Once more, what news?
DERBY   Richmond is on the seas.
KING RICHARD
  There let him sink, and be the seas on him!
  White-livered renegade, what doth he there?   464
DERBY
  I know not, mighty sovereign, but by guess.
KING RICHARD
  Well, as you guess?
DERBY
  Stirred up by Dorset, Buckingham, and Morton,

---

455 *post* hasten 464 *White-livered* cowardly

He makes for England, here to claim the crown.

KING RICHARD

469   Is the chair empty? Is the sword unswayed?
470   Is the king dead? The empire unpossessed?
      What heir of York is there alive but we?
      And who is England's king but great York's heir?
473   Then tell me, what makes he upon the seas?

DERBY

      Unless for that, my liege, I cannot guess.

KING RICHARD

      Unless for that he comes to be your liege,
      You cannot guess wherefore the Welshman comes.
      Thou wilt revolt and fly to him, I fear.

DERBY

      No, my good lord; therefore mistrust me not.

KING RICHARD

      Where is thy power then to beat him back?
480   Where be thy tenants and thy followers?
      Are they not now upon the western shore,
      Safe-conducting the rebels from their ships?

DERBY

      No, my good lord, my friends are in the north.

KING RICHARD

484   Cold friends to me! What do they in the north
      When they should serve their sovereign in the west?

DERBY

      They have not been commanded, mighty king.
      Pleaseth your majesty to give me leave,
      I'll muster up my friends and meet your grace
      Where and what time your majesty shall please.

KING RICHARD

490   Ay, ay, thou wouldst be gone to join with Richmond.

---

469 *sword* i.e., the sword of state, part of the king's regalia symbolic of power
470 *empire* kingdom (i.e., the thing requiring rule)   473 *makes he* is he
doing 484 *Cold* chilling (with play on Derby's friends being in the *north*)

But I'll not trust thee.
DERBY   Most mighty sovereign,
  You have no cause to hold my friendship doubtful.
  I never was nor never will be false.
KING RICHARD
  Go then and muster men. But leave behind
  Your son, George Stanley. Look your heart be firm,
  Or else his head's assurance is but frail.   496
DERBY
  So deal with him as I prove true to you.   *Exit.*
    Enter a Messenger.
FIRST MESSENGER
  My gracious sovereign, now in Devonshire,
  As I by friends am well advertisèd,   499
  Sir Edward Courtney and the haughty prelate,   500
  Bishop of Exeter, his elder brother,
  With many more confederates, are in arms.
    Enter another Messenger.
SECOND MESSENGER
  In Kent, my liege, the Guildfords are in arms,
  And every hour more competitors
  Flock to the rebels, and their power grows strong.
    Enter another Messenger.
THIRD MESSENGER
  My lord, the army of great Buckingham –
KING RICHARD
  Out on ye, owls! Nothing but songs of death?   507
    He striketh him.
  There, take thou that, till thou bring better news.
THIRD MESSENGER
  The news I have to tell your majesty
  Is that by sudden floods and fall of waters   510
  Buckingham's army is dispersed and scattered,

---

496 *head's assurance* i.e., that his head will not be cut off 499 *advertisèd* informed 500, 503 *Courtney, Guildfords* (supporters of Buckingham) 507 *owls* (the hoot or song of the owl was frequently believed to portend evil)

And he himself wandered away alone,
513   No man knows whither.
KING RICHARD   I cry thee mercy.
There is my purse to cure that blow of thine.
515   Hath any well-advisèd friend proclaimed
Reward to him that brings the traitor in?
THIRD MESSENGER
Such proclamation hath been made, my lord.
        Enter another Messenger.
FOURTH MESSENGER
518   Sir Thomas Lovel and Lord Marquess Dorset,
'Tis said, my liege, in Yorkshire are in arms.
520   But this good comfort bring I to your highness:
The Breton navy is dispersed by tempest;
Richmond in Dorsetshire sent out a boat
Unto the shore to ask those on the banks
If they were his assistants, yea or no,
Who answered him they came from Buckingham
Upon his party. He, mistrusting them,
527   Hoist sail, and made his course again for Bretagne.
KING RICHARD
March on, march on, since we are up in arms,
If not to fight with foreign enemies,
530   Yet to beat down these rebels here at home.
        Enter Catesby.
CATESBY
My liege, the Duke of Buckingham is taken.
That is the best news. That the Earl of Richmond
533   Is with a mighty power landed at Milford
Is colder tidings, but yet they must be told.
KING RICHARD
Away towards Salisbury! While we reason here,
A royal battle might be won and lost.

---

513 *cry thee mercy* beg your pardon   515 *well-advisèd* foresighted   518
Lovel (supporter of Buckingham)   527 *Bretagne* Brittany   533 *Milford* Milford Haven, a port on the Welsh coast

Some one take order Buckingham be brought
To Salisbury. The rest march on with me.

Flourish. Exeunt.

*

❧ **IV.5** *Enter [Lord Stanley Earl of] Derby, and Sir
Christopher [Urswick, a priest].*

DERBY
Sir Christopher, tell Richmond this from me:
That in the sty of the most deadly boar
My son George Stanley is franked up in hold.   3
If I revolt, off goes young George's head;
The fear of that holds off my present aid.
So get thee gone; commend me to thy lord.
Withal say that the queen hath heartily consented
He should espouse Elizabeth her daughter.
But tell me, where is princely Richmond now?

CHRISTOPHER
At Pembroke, or at Ha'rfordwest in Wales.   10

DERBY
What men of name resort to him?

CHRISTOPHER
Sir Walter Herbert, a renownèd soldier,
Sir Gilbert Talbot, Sir William Stanley,   13
Oxford, redoubted Pembroke, Sir James Blunt,   14
And Rhys-ap-Thomas, with a valiant crew,
And many other of great name and worth;
And towards London do they bend their power,
If by the way they be not fought withal.

IV.5 Possibly in Lord Stanley's house **s.d.** *Sir* (see III.2.109) **3** *franked up in
hold* shut up (as in a *sty*, l. 2) in custody (the *boar* in l. 2 being, of course,
Richard) **10** *Pembroke* a county in southwestern Wales (see reference to the
Pembroke family, l. 14); *Ha'rfordwest* Haverford West, a town in Pem-
brokeshire on Milford Haven **13** *Sir William Stanley* (Derby's brother) **14**
redoubted dreaded; *Pembroke* i.e., Jasper Tudor, Richmond's uncle

DERBY
    Well, hie thee to thy lord. I kiss his hand.
20 My letter will resolve him of my mind.
        [Gives letter.]
    Farewell.   Exeunt.

                          *

∾ V.1 *Enter Buckingham with Halberds [and the
    Sheriff], led to execution.*

BUCKINGHAM
    Will not King Richard let me speak with him?
SHERIFF
    No, my good lord; therefore be patient.
BUCKINGHAM
    Hastings, and Edward's children, Grey and Rivers,
    Holy King Henry and thy fair son Edward,
    Vaughan and all that have miscarrièd
    By underhand, corrupted, foul injustice,
7   If that your moody discontented souls
    Do through the clouds behold this present hour,
9   Even for revenge mock my destruction.
10 This is All Souls' Day, fellow, is it not?
SHERIFF
    It is, my lord.
BUCKINGHAM
12 Why, then All Souls' Day is my body's doomsday.
    This is the day which in King Edward's time
    I wished might fall on me when I was found
    False to his children and his wife's allies.
    This is the day wherein I wished to fall
    By the false faith of him whom most I trusted.

V.1 *Salisbury* 7 *moody* angry; *discontented souls* i.e., souls that could not
rest in peace until their violent deaths had been revenged 9 *Even for* i.e., im-
pelled by 10 *All Souls' Day* November 2, the day on which the Roman
Catholic Church intercedes for all Christian souls 12 *doomsday* day of final
judgment (death being the sentence)

This, this All Souls' Day to my fearful soul   18
Is the determined respite of my wrongs.   19
That high All-seer which I dallied with   20
Hath turned my feignèd prayer on my head
And given in earnest what I begged in jest.
Thus doth he force the swords of wicked men
To turn their own points in their masters' bosoms.
Thus Margaret's curse falls heavy on my neck.
"When he," quoth she, "shall split thy heart with sorrow,
Remember Margaret was a prophetess." –
Come lead me, officers, to the block of shame.
Wrong hath but wrong, and blame the due of blame.

> *Exeunt.*

*

❧ **V.2** *Enter [Henry Earl of] Richmond, [the Earl of]
Oxford, [Sir James] Blunt, [Sir Walter] Herbert, and
others, with Drum and Colors.*

RICHMOND

Fellows in arms, and my most loving friends,
Bruised underneath the yoke of tyranny,
Thus far into the bowels of the land   3
Have we marched on without impediment;
And here receive we from our father Stanley   5
Lines of fair comfort and encouragement.
The wretched, bloody, and usurping boar,
That spoiled your summer fields and fruitful vines,
Swills your warm blood like wash, and makes his trough

---

18 *fearful* terrified **19** *determined . . . wrongs* i.e., the foreordained moment
to which punishment of my sins has been postponed

V.2 Tamworth, Staffordshire **3** *bowels* heart or center (Richmond's army
is on its way to the scene of the final battle with Richard at Bosworth Field,
Leicestershire; cf. ll. 12–13) **5** *our* (royal plural); *father Stanley* (Richmond
was the son of Edmund Tudor and Margaret Beaufort; Lord Stanley, Earl of
Derby, was his mother's third husband, Richmond's stepfather)

10   In your emboweled bosoms – this foul swine
11   Is now even in the centry of this isle,
      Near to the town of Leicester, as we learn.
      From Tamworth thither is but one day's march.
      In God's name cheerly on, courageous friends,
      To reap the harvest of perpetual peace
      By this one bloody trial of sharp war.

OXFORD
17   Every man's conscience is a thousand men,
      To fight against this guilty homicide.

HERBERT
      I doubt not but his friends will turn to us.

BLUNT
20   He hath no friends but what are friends for fear,
      Which in his dearest need will fly from him.

RICHMOND
      All for our vantage. Then, in God's name, march.
      True hope is swift and flies with swallow's wings;
      Kings it makes gods, and meaner creatures kings.
                                        ⸜ Exeunt omnes.

                          *

∾ **V.3** *Enter King Richard in arms, with Norfolk,*
      Ratcliffe, and the Earl of Surrey [, and Soldiers].

KING RICHARD
      Here pitch our tent, even here in Bosworth field.
      [Soldiers begin to set up the King's tent.]
2   My Lord of Surrey, why look you so sad?

SURREY
      My heart is ten times lighter than my looks.

KING RICHARD
      My Lord of Norfolk –

---

10 *emboweled* disemboweled 11 *centry* center 17 *conscience* i.e., his conscience tells him that he is on the "right" side
      V.3 Bosworth Field 2 *sad* heavy-spirited

NORFOLK   Here, most gracious liege.

KING RICHARD
  Norfolk, we must have knocks. Ha, must we not?

NORFOLK
  We must both give and take, my loving lord.

KING RICHARD
  Up with my tent! Here will I lie tonight.
  But where tomorrow? Well, all's one for that.   8
  Who hath descried the number of the traitors?

NORFOLK
  Six or seven thousand is their utmost power.   10

KING RICHARD
  Why, our battalia trebles that account.   11
  Besides, the king's name is a tower of strength,
  Which they upon the adverse faction want.   13
  Up with the tent! Come, noble gentlemen,
  Let us survey the vantage of the ground.   15
  Call for some men of sound direction.   16
  Let's lack no discipline, make no delay,
  For, lords, tomorrow is a busy day.   *Exeunt.*   18
      Enter Richmond, Sir William Brandon, Oxford, and
      Dorset [, Herbert, and Blunt and others. Some of the
      Soldiers pitch Richmond's tent].

RICHMOND
  The weary sun hath made a golden set
  And by the bright track of his fiery car   20
  Gives token of a goodly day tomorrow.
  Sir William Brandon, you shall bear my standard.
  Give me some ink and paper in my tent:

---

8 *all's . . . that* i.e., it makes no difference 11 *battalia* armed forces 13
want lack 15 *the vantage . . . ground* i.e., the military advantages offered by
the spot chosen for the battle 16 *of sound direction* capable of giving sound
orders 18 s.d. *Exeunt* (Some editors mark a new scene at this point with the
clear stage. It is not sure whether there needs to be a second tent pitched onstage for this and subsequent scenes; if there is a second one, Richmond's soldiers start to pitch it at this point.) 20 *car* chariot (with reference to the
chariot of Phoebus, god of the sun)

I'll draw the form and model of our battle,
Limit each leader to his several charge,
And part in just proportion our small power.
My Lord of Oxford, – you, Sir William Brandon, –
And you, Sir Walter Herbert – stay with me.
29   The Earl of Pembroke keeps his regiment;
30   Good Captain Blunt, bear my good-night to him,
And by the second hour in the morning
Desire the earl to see me in my tent.
Yet one thing more, good captain, do for me –
Where is Lord Stanley quartered, do you know?

BLUNT
Unless I have mista'en his colors much,
Which well I am assured I have not done,
His regiment lies half a mile at least
South from the mighty power of the king.

RICHMOND
If without peril it be possible,
40   Sweet Blunt, make some good means to speak with him
And give him from me this most needful note.
    [Hands him a letter.]

BLUNT
Upon my life, my lord, I'll undertake it;
And so God give you quiet rest tonight!

RICHMOND
Good night, good Captain Blunt.   *[Exit Blunt.]*
                            Come, gentlemen,
Let us consult upon tomorrow's business.
46   In to my tent; the dew is raw and cold.
    They withdraw into the tent.
    Enter [, to his tent, King] Richard, Ratcliffe, Norfolk,
    and Catesby [and others].

KING RICHARD
What is't o'clock?

CATESBY   It's suppertime, my lord.

---

29 *keeps* stays with 46 s.d. *They . . . tent* (Again, the clear stage prompts
some editors to mark a new scene here.)

It's nine o'clock.   48
KING RICHARD   I will not sup tonight.
Give me some ink and paper.
What, is my beaver easier than it was?   50
And all my armor laid into my tent?
CATESBY
It is, my liege, and all things are in readiness.
KING RICHARD
Good Norfolk, hie thee to thy charge.
Use careful watch, choose trusty sentinels.   54
NORFOLK
I go, my lord.
KING RICHARD
Stir with the lark tomorrow, gentle Norfolk.
NORFOLK
I warrant you, my lord.   *Exit.*
KING RICHARD
Catesby!
CATESBY
My lord?   59
KING RICHARD   Send out a pursuivant-at-arms
To Stanley's regiment. Bid him bring his power   60
Before sunrising, lest his son George fall
Into the blind cave of eternal night.   *[Exit Catesby.]*
Fill me a bowl of wine. Give me a watch.   63
Saddle white Surrey for the field tomorrow.   64
Look that my staves be sound and not too heavy.   65
Ratcliffe!
RATCLIFFE
My lord?

---

48 *nine o'clock* (too late for an Elizabethan supper; the "six of clocke" of Q fits this context better) **50** *beaver* face guard of a helmet; *easier* freer in movement **54** *Use careful watch* i.e., see that a thorough alert is observed **59** *pursuivant-at-arms* junior officer, attending on a herald **63** *a watch* a special guard (cf. l. 77) or a timepiece **64** *white Surrey* (Richard entered Leicester on a "great white courser" [Holinshed], but the name is Shakespeare's and must not be confused with *Surrey* in l. 69) **65** *staves* lance shafts

KING RICHARD
    Saw'st thou the melancholy Lord Northumberland?
RATCLIFFE
    Thomas the Earl of Surrey and himself,
70   Much about cockshut time, from troop to troop
    Went through the army, cheering up the soldiers.
KING RICHARD
    So, I am satisfied. Give me a bowl of wine.
    I have not that alacrity of spirit
    Nor cheer of mind that I was wont to have.
      [Wine brought.]
    Set it down. Is ink and paper ready?
RATCLIFFE
    It is, my lord.
KING RICHARD
    Bid my guard watch. Leave me. Ratcliffe,
    About the mid of night come to my tent
79   And help to arm me. Leave me, I say.   *Exit Ratcliffe.*
      [King Richard sleeps.]
      Enter [Lord Stanley Earl of] Derby, to Richmond in
      his tent [, Lords and others attending].
DERBY
80   Fortune and victory sit on thy helm!
RICHMOND
    All comfort that the dark night can afford
    Be to thy person, noble father-in-law!
    Tell me, how fares our loving mother?
DERBY
84   I, by attorney, bless thee from thy mother,
    Who prays continually for Richmond's good:
    So much for that. The silent hours steal on
87   And flaky darkness breaks within the east.
    In brief, for so the season bids us be,

---

70 *cockshut time* evening twilight 79 s.d. *Exit . . . attending* (if there were
two tents, Richard presumably sleeps at the entrance to his) 84 *attorney*
proxy 87 *flaky darkness* i.e., darkness still flaked with light

Prepare thy battle early in the morning   89
And put thy fortune to the arbitrament   90
Of bloody strokes and mortal-staring war.   91
I, as I may – that which I would I cannot –
With best advantage will deceive the time   93
And aid thee in this doubtful shock of arms.
But on thy side I may not be too forward,
Lest, being seen, thy brother, tender George,
Be executed in his father's sight.
Farewell. The leisure and the fearful time   98
Cuts off the ceremonious vows of love
And ample interchange of sweet discourse   *100*
Which so long sundered friends should dwell upon.
God give us leisure for these rites of love.
Once more adieu. Be valiant, and speed well!

RICHMOND
Good lords, conduct him to his regiment.
I'll strive with troubled thoughts to take a nap,   105
Lest leaden slumber peise me down tomorrow,   106
When I should mount with wings of victory.
Once more, good night, kind lords and gentlemen.
                            Exeunt. Manet Richmond.
O Thou, whose captain I account myself,
Look on my forces with a gracious eye;   *110*
Put in their hands thy bruising irons of wrath,   111
That they may crush down with a heavy fall
Th' usurping helmets of our adversaries;
Make us thy ministers of chastisement,
That we may praise thee in the victory.
To thee I do commend my watchful soul
Ere I let fall the windows of mine eyes,   117
Sleeping and waking. O, defend me still!

---

89 *battle* armed forces (see *battalia,* l. 11 above) 90 *arbitrament* judgment
91 *mortal-staring* killing (like the basilisk) with a glance of the eye 93
With . . . time i.e., will make the greatest profit of the moment without giving the appearance of doing so 98 *leisure . . . time* (lack of) time and the
threat of the moment 105 *with* in spite of 106 *peise* weigh 111 *irons*
swords 117 *windows* i.e., eyelids

Sleeps.
Enter the Ghost of Prince Edward, son to Henry
the Sixth.

GHOST *To Richard*
Let me sit heavy on thy soul tomorrow,

120 Think how thou stab'st me in my prime of youth
At Tewkesbury. Despair therefore, and die.
To Richmond

122 Be cheerful, Richmond, for the wrongèd souls
Of butchered princes fight in thy behalf.

124 King Henry's issue, Richmond, comforts thee.   *[Exit.]*
Enter the Ghost of Henry the Sixth.

GHOST *To Richard*
125 When I was mortal, my anointed body
By thee was punchèd full of deadly holes.

127 Think on the Tower, and me. Despair, and die.
Harry the Sixth bids thee despair and die!
To Richmond
Virtuous and holy, be thou conqueror.

130 Harry, that prophesied thou shouldst be king,
Doth comfort thee in thy sleep. Live and flourish!

[Exit.]

Enter the Ghost of Clarence.
GHOST *[To Richard]*
Let me sit heavy in thy soul tomorrow,

133 I that was washed to death with fulsome wine,
Poor Clarence by thy guile betrayed to death.
Tomorrow in the battle think on me,

136 And fall thy edgeless sword. Despair, and die!
To Richmond

---

122 *cheerful* full of joy 124 **s.d.** *Exit* (No early text marks exits for this and
the other ghosts. They might accumulate onstage and exeunt together at l.
177, but it is more likely, especially with doubling, that each leaves after
speaking.) 125 *anointed* (as king at his coronation, see IV.1.61n.) 127
Tower (of London, where Richard killed Henry VI) 130 *Harry . . . king* (see
Henry VI, Part 3, IV.7.67–76) 133 *fulsome* sickening or satiating 136
fall . . . sword i.e., let thy blunted sword fall

Thou offspring of the house of Lancaster,   137
The wrongèd heirs of York do pray for thee;
Good angels guard thy battle. Live and flourish! *[Exit.]*
    Enter the Ghosts of Rivers, Grey, and Vaughan.
GHOST OF RIVERS   *[To Richard]*
Let me sit heavy in thy soul tomorrow,   140
Rivers, that died at Pomfret. Despair and dïe!
GHOST OF GREY
Think upon Grey, and let thy soul despair!
GHOST OF VAUGHAN
Think upon Vaughan, and with guilty fear
Let fall thy lance. Despair and die!
ALL GHOSTS   *To Richmond*
Awake, and think our wrongs in Richard's bosom
Will conquer him. Awake, and win the day!
                                            [Exeunt Ghosts.]

    Enter the Ghost of Lord Hastings.
GHOST   *[To Richard]*
Bloody and guilty, guiltily awake
And in a bloody battle end thy days.
Think on Lord Hastings. Despair and die!
    To Richmond
Quiet untroubled soul, awake, awake!   150
Arm, fight, and conquer, for fair England's sake!   *[Exit.]*
    Enter the Ghosts of the two young Princes.
GHOSTS   *[To Richard]*
Dream on thy cousins smothered in the Tower.   152
Let us be lead within thy bosom, Richard,
And weigh thee down to ruin, shame, and death.
Thy nephews' souls bid thee despair and die!
    To Richmond
Sleep, Richmond, sleep in peace and wake in joy.
Good angels guard thee from the boar's annoy.   157

---

137 *offspring . . . Lancaster* (Richmond's mother was a Beaufort, and the
Beaufort line traced back to John of Gaunt, Duke of Lancaster, the father
of Bolingbroke, who became Henry IV)   152 *cousins* kinsmen (here, nephews)
157 *annoy* molestation

Live, and beget a happy race of kings!
Edward's unhappy sons do bid thee flourish.

[Exeunt Ghosts.]

Enter the Ghost of Anne, his wife.

GHOST   *To Richard*

160 Richard, thy wife, that wretched Anne thy wife,
That never slept a quiet hour with thee,
Now fills thy sleep with perturbations.
Tomorrow in the battle think on me,
And fall thy edgeless sword. Despair and die!

To Richmond

Thou quiet soul, sleep thou a quiet sleep.
Dream of success and happy victory.
Thy adversary's wife doth pray for thee.   *[Exit.]*

Enter the Ghost of Buckingham.

GHOST   *To Richard*

The first was I that helped thee to the crown;
The last was I that felt thy tyranny.

170 O, in the battle think on Buckingham,
And die in terror of thy guiltiness!
Dream on, dream on, of bloody deeds and death;
Fainting, despair; despairing, yield thy breath.

To Richmond

174 I died for hope ere I could lend thee aid.
But cheer thy heart and be thou not dismayed.
God and good angels fight on Richmond's side,
And Richard falls in height of all his pride.   *[Exit.]*

Richard starteth up out of a dream.

KING RICHARD

Give me another horse! Bind up my wounds!
Have mercy, Jesu – Soft! I did but dream.

180 O coward conscience, how dost thou afflict me.
The lights burn blue. It is now dead midnight.
Cold fearful drops stand on my trembling flesh.
What do I fear? Myself? There's none else by.

---

174 *for hope* while hoping

Richard loves Richard; that is, I and I.   184
Is there a murderer here? No. Yes, I am.
Then fly. What, from myself? Great reason why –
Lest I revenge. What, myself upon myself?
Alack, I love myself. Wherefore? For any good
That I myself have done unto myself?
O no, alas, I rather hate myself   190
For hateful deeds committed by myself.
I am a villain. Yet I lie: I am not.
Fool, of thyself speak well. Fool, do not flatter.
My conscience hath a thousand several tongues,   194
And every tongue brings in a several tale,
And every tale condemns me for a villain.
Perjury, perjury, in the highest degree,
Murder, stern murder, in the direst degree,
All several sins, all used in each degree,   199
Throng to the bar, crying all, "Guilty, guilty!"   200
I shall despair. There is no creature loves me;
And if I die, no soul will pity me.
And wherefore should they, since that I myself
Find in myself no pity to myself?
Methought the souls of all that I had murdered
Came to my tent, and every one did threat
Tomorrow's vengeance on the head of Richard.
    Enter Ratcliffe.

RATCLIFFE
  My lord!
KING RICHARD
  Zounds, who is there?
RATCLIFFE
  Ratcliffe, my lord, 'tis I. The early village cock   210
  Hath twice done salutation to the morn:

---

184 *I and I* (this reading, from Q, has usually been rejected by editors in
favor of Q2's "I am I"; see Introduction, p. xxxvi) 194 *several* separate 199
All . . . degree all kinds of sins, each one practiced in all its comparative stages
(e.g., bad, worse, worst; cf. ll. 197–98) 200 *bar* (of the law court)

Your friends are up and buckle on their armor.

KING RICHARD

O Ratcliffe, I have dreamed a fearful dream!
What think'st thou? Will our friends prove all true?

RATCLIFFE

No doubt, my lord.

KING RICHARD   O Ratcliffe, I fear, I fear!

RATCLIFFE

Nay, good my lord, be not afraid of shadows.

KING RICHARD

By the apostle Paul, shadows tonight
Have struck more terror to the soul of Richard
Than can the substance of ten thousand soldiers
220   Armèd in proof and led by shallow Richmond.
'Tis not yet near day. Come, go with me.
Under our tents I'll play the eavesdropper,
To see if any mean to shrink from me.

> *Exeunt Richard and Ratcliffe.*
> *Enter the Lords to Richmond sitting in his tent.*

LORD

224   Good morrow, Richmond.

RICHMOND

225   Cry mercy, lords and watchful gentlemen,
That you have ta'en a tardy sluggard here.

LORD

How have you slept, my lord?

RICHMOND

228   The sweetest sleep and fairest-boding dreams
That ever entered in a drowsy head
230   Have I since your departure had, my lords.
Methought their souls whose bodies Richard murdered
232   Came to my tent and cried on victory.
233   I promise you my soul is very jocund

---

220 *in proof* impenetrable **224** *lord* (the speech prefix of Q, "Lo," is am-
biguous; a single speaker seems preferable here and at 227, 236) **225** *Cry
mercy* beg pardon **228** *fairest-boding* most propitious **232** *cried on* invoked
233 *jocund* joyful

In the remembrance of so fair a dream.
How far into the morning is it, lords?

LORD

Upon the stroke of four.

RICHMOND

Why, then 'tis time to arm and give direction.
His Oration to his Soldiers.
More than I have said, loving countrymen,
The leisure and enforcement of the time   239
Forbids to dwell upon. Yet remember this: 240
God and our good cause fight upon our side;
The prayers of holy saints and wrongèd souls,
Like high-reared bulwarks, stand before our faces.   243
Richard except, those whom we fight against
Had rather have us win than him they follow.
For what is he they follow? Truly, gentlemen,
A bloody tyrant and a homicide;
One raised in blood and one in blood established;   248
One that made means to come by what he hath,   249
And slaughtered those that were the means to help   250
  him;
A base foul stone, made precious by the foil   251
Of England's chair, where he is falsely set;
One that hath ever been God's enemy.
Then if you fight against God's enemy,
God will in justice ward you as his soldiers;   255
If you do sweat to put a tyrant down,
You sleep in peace, the tyrant being slain;
If you do fight against your country's foes,
Your country's fat shall pay your pains the hire;   259

---

239 *leisure* (see l. 98)   **243** *bulwarks* defensive ramparts   **248** *One . . . established* i.e., one who came to the throne through bloodshed and has held it
through further bloodshed (this is the theme of Richmond's justification for
deposing Richard)   **249** *One . . . means* i.e., one who did not let events take
their natural course but engineered them to his advantage   **251** *foil* metal
leaf (*England's chair* or throne) placed under a jewel (*stone*, Richard) to make
it appear more brilliant than it is   **255** *ward* protect   **259** *fat* abundant fer-
tility

260   If you do fight in safeguard of your wives,
        Your wives shall welcome home the conquerors;
        If you do free your children from the sword,
263   Your children's children quits it in your age:
        Then in the name of God and all these rights,
        Advance your standards, draw your willing swords.
266   For me, the ransom of my bold attempt
        Shall be this cold corpse on the earth's cold face;
        But if I thrive, the gain of my attempt
        The least of you shall share his part thereof.
270   Sound drums and trumpets boldly and cheerfully:
271   God and Saint George! Richmond and victory!
                       [Exeunt. Drums and trumpets sound.]
        Enter King Richard, Ratcliffe [, and Soldiers].

KING RICHARD
     What said Northumberland as touching Richmond?

RATCLIFFE
     That he was never trainèd up in arms.

KING RICHARD
     He said the truth. And what said Surrey then?

RATCLIFFE
     He smiled and said, "The better for our purpose."

KING RICHARD
     He was in the right, and so indeed it is.
       The clock striketh.

277   Tell the clock there. Give me a calendar.
       [He is given a book.]
       Who saw the sun today?

RATCLIFFE   Not I, my lord.

KING RICHARD
     Then he disdains to shine, for by the book
280   He should have braved the east an hour ago.
        A black day will it be to somebody.

---

263 *quits* requites **266–67** *the ransom . . . face* i.e., (if we fail), my only ransom (freeing from captivity) will be by death **271 s.d.** *Exeunt . . . sound* (some editors mark a new scene here after the clear stage; I have kept to the traditional scene divisions) **277** *Tell* count; *calendar* almanac

Ratcliffe!

RATCLIFFE
My lord?

KING RICHARD   The sun will not be seen today;
The sky doth frown and lower upon our army.   284
I would these dewy tears were from the ground.   285
Not shine today? Why, what is that to me
More than to Richmond? For the selfsame heaven
That frowns on me looks sadly upon him.
   Enter Norfolk.

NORFOLK
Arm, arm, my lord! The foe vaunts in the field.

KING RICHARD
Come, bustle, bustle! Caparison my horse!   290
Call up Lord Stanley, bid him bring his power.
                                                            [Exit one.]
I will lead forth my soldiers to the plain,
And thus my battle shall be orderèd:
My foreward shall be drawn out all in length,
Consisting equally of horse and foot;
Our archers shall be placèd in the midst;
John Duke of Norfolk, Thomas Earl of Surrey,
Shall have the leading of this foot and horse.
They thus directed, we will follow   299
In the main battle, whose puissance on either side   300
Shall be well wingèd with our chiefest horse.   301
This, and Saint George to boot! What think'st thou,   302
   Norfolk?

NORFOLK
A good direction, warlike sovereign.
This found I on my tent this morning.
   He showeth him a paper.

---

284 *lower* glower (see I.1.3) **285** *dewy tears* i.e., morning dew (*tears* because the sky frowns, l. 284) **290** *Come . . . horse* (Richard may put on his
armor at this point); *Caparison* cover with a rich horsecloth **299** *directed*
placed tactically **300** *puissance* force or power **301** *well wingèd . . . horse*
i.e., the best horsemen will be well deployed as wings (on either side of the
main body of troops; cf. *main battle,* l. 300) **302** *to boot* as a helper

305 "Jockey of Norfolk, be not so bold,
306 For Dickon thy master is bought and sold."

KING RICHARD

 A thing devisèd by the enemy.
 Go, gentlemen, every man unto his charge.
 Let not our babbling dreams affright our souls.
310 Conscience is but a word that cowards use,
 Devised at first to keep the strong in awe.
312 Our strong arms be our conscience, swords our law!
313 March on, join bravely, let us to it pell-mell,
 If not to heaven, then hand in hand to hell.

   His Oration to his Army.

315 What shall I say more than I have inferred?
316 Remember whom you are to cope withal:
317 A sort of vagabonds, rascals, and runaways,
318 A scum of Bretons and base lackey peasants,
319 Whom their o'ercloyèd country vomits forth
320 To desperate adventures and assured destruction.
 You sleeping safe, they bring to you unrest;
 You having lands, and blessed with beauteous wives,
323 They would restrain the one, distain the other.
 And who doth lead them but a paltry fellow,
325 Long kept in Bretagne at our mother's cost,
 A milksop, one that never in his life
327 Felt so much cold as over shoes in snow.
 Let's whip these stragglers o'er the seas again,
 Lash hence these overweening rags of France,
330 These famished beggars, weary of their lives,
331 Who, but for dreaming on this fond exploit,
332 For want of means, poor rats, had hanged themselves.
 If we be conquered, let men conquer us,

---

305 *Jockey* i.e., John or Jack (familiar form) 306 *Dickon* i.e., Richard or Dick (familiar form) 312 *strong . . . conscience* i.e., might makes right 313 *join* join battle 315 *inferred* reported 316 *cope withal* meet with 317 *sort* band 318 *lackey* lowbred 319 *o'ercloyèd* overfull 323 *restrain* deprive you of; *distain* dishonor, sully 325 *Bretagne* Brittany 327 *over . . . snow* i.e., snow deeper than shoe level 331 *but for* if it were not for; *fond* foolish 332 *means* the wherewithal to live

And not these bastard Bretons, whom our fathers
Have in their own land beaten, bobbed, and thumped,
And, in record, left them the heirs of shame.
Shall these enjoy our lands? lie with our wives?
Ravish our daughters?
 Drum afar off. Hark, I hear their drum.
Fight, gentlemen of England! Fight, bold yeomen!
Draw, archers, draw your arrows to the head!   *340*
Spur your proud horses hard, and ride in blood!   *341*
Amaze the welkin with your broken staves!   *342*
 Enter a Messenger.
What says Lord Stanley? Will he bring his power?

MESSENGER
My lord, he doth deny to come.   *344*

KING RICHARD
Off with his son George's head!

NORFOLK
My lord, the enemy is past the marsh.
After the battle let George Stanley die.

KING RICHARD
A thousand hearts are great within my bosom.
Advance our standards, set upon our foes.
Our ancient word of courage, fair Saint George,   *350*
Inspire us with the spleen of fiery dragons.   *351*
Upon them! Victory sits on our helms.   *[Exeunt.]*

*

∽ **V.4** *Alarum. Excursions. Enter Catesby.*

CATESBY *[Calling]*
Rescue, my Lord of Norfolk, rescue, rescue!
The king enacts more wonders than a man,

---

341 *in blood* (1) in full vigor (a hunting term), (2) smeared with blood from
spurring   342 *welkin* sky; *staves* lance shafts   344 *deny* refuse   350 *word*
battle cry   351 *spleen* fiery temper
 V.4 s.d. *Alarum . . . Catesby* (editors have usually marked an entrance for
Norfolk and soldiers here, but Catesby could just as easily be calling offstage)

3 Daring an opposite to every danger.
His horse is slain, and all on foot he fights,
Seeking for Richmond in the throat of death.
Rescue, fair lord, or else the day is lost!
  Alarums. Enter [King] Richard.

KING RICHARD

7 A horse, a horse! My kingdom for a horse!

CATESBY

Withdraw, my lord. I'll help you to a horse.

KING RICHARD

9 Slave, I have set my life upon a cast,
10 And I will stand the hazard of the die.
11 I think there be six Richmonds in the field;
Five have I slain today instead of him.
A horse, a horse! My kingdom for a horse! *[Exeunt.]*

       *

∾ **V.5** *Alarum. Enter [King] Richard and Richmond;
they fight; Richard is slain. [Exit Richmond. Richard's
body is carried off.] Then retreat being sounded.
[Flourish.] Enter Richmond, [Lord Stanley Earl of]
Derby, bearing the crown, with divers other Lords
[and Soldiers].*

RICHMOND

God and your arms be praised, victorious friends!
The day is ours; the bloody dog is dead.

---

3 *Daring an opposite* offering himself as an opponent 7 *A horse ... horse*
(Cf. *The True Tragedie of Richard III:* "A horse, a horse, a fresh horse." It
seems likely that Shakespeare derived his famous line from this rather flat
hint.) 9 *cast* throw (of the dice) 10 *die* (singular of dice) 11 *six Richmonds* i.e., in addition to Richmond, five other men dressed and armed to re-
semble Richmond (a common safety measure)

 V.5 s.d. *Richard's ... off* (the corpse could stay onstage, but it is more
likely to have been carried off so that Stanley can enter carrying the crown);
retreat a trumpet signal for Richard's men to retire

DERBY

  Courageous Richmond, well hast thou acquit thee.

  Lo, here this long usurpèd royalty

  From the dead temples of this bloody wretch

  Have I plucked off, to grace thy brows withal.

  Wear it, enjoy it, and make much of it.

    [Derby crowns Richmond.]

RICHMOND

  Great God of heaven, say amen to all!

  But tell me, is young George Stanley living?

DERBY

  He is, my lord, and safe in Leicester town,   *10*

  Whither, if it please you, we may now withdraw us.

RICHMOND

  What men of name are slain on either side?

DERBY

  John Duke of Norfolk, Walter Lord Ferrers,

  Sir Robert Brakenbury, and Sir William Brandon.

RICHMOND

  Inter their bodies as become their births.

  Proclaim a pardon to the soldiers fled

  That in submission will return to us,

  And then, as we have ta'en the sacrament,   *18*

  We will unite the White Rose and the Red.   *19*

  Smile heaven upon this fair conjunction,   *20*

  That long have frowned upon their enmity.

  What traitor hears me and says not amen?

  England hath long been mad and scarred herself;

---

18 *as . . . sacrament* (referring to the oath, taken by Richmond in the cathedral at Rheims, that he would marry Princess Elizabeth as soon as he was possessed of the crown) **19** *White Rose . . . Red* i.e., the badges of the Yorkist and Lancastrian factions, respectively; the marriage of Richmond (Lancastrian) and Princess Elizabeth (Yorkist) will bring an end to the so-called Wars of the Roses (see ll. 27–31) **20** *conjunction* marriage union (with play on the astrological meaning: the sun [the king symbol: Richmond] and Venus [Elizabeth] will be "in conjunction" – i.e., in the same sign of the zodiac at the same time)

The brother blindly shed the brother's blood;
25 The father rashly slaughtered his own son;
The son, compelled, been butcher to the sire.
All this divided York and Lancaster,
Divided in their dire division,
O, now let Richmond and Elizabeth,
30 The true succeeders of each royal house,
By God's fair ordinance conjoin together.
And let their heirs – God, if thy will be so –
Enrich the time to come with smooth-faced peace,
With smiling plenty, and fair prosperous days.
35 Abate the edge of traitors, gracious Lord,
36 That would reduce these bloody days again
And make poor England weep in streams of blood.
Let them not live to taste this land's increase
That would with treason wound this fair land's peace.
40 Now civil wounds are stopped, peace lives again:
That she may long live here, God say amen.

                                        Exeunt.

25–26 *The father . . . sire* (Shakespeare seems to be recalling *Henry VI, Part 3*, II.5) **35** *Abate the edge* i.e., blunt the sharpness (of traitors' swords) **36** *reduce* bring back

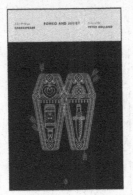

AVALIABLE FROM PENGUIN CLASSICS

THE PELICAN SHAKESPEARE

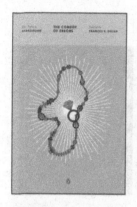

The Comedy of Errors • Coriolanus • Henry VI, Part 1

Henry VIII • Love's Labor's Lost • The Two Gentlemen of Verona

General Editors: Stephen Orgel and A. R. Braunmuller

New Illustrated Covers designed by Manuja Waldia

P.O. 0005374661 20230822